BOWMAN LIBRA
MENLO SCHOOL AND MENLO COLLEGE

P9-CKT-548

MENLO SCHOOL
founded 1915
MENLO COLLEGE
Gift of
College Student Council
Library Fund
Established Fall of 1972

EAKINS

EAKINS

by SYLVAN SCHENDLER

LITTLE, BROWN AND COMPANY · BOSTON · TORONTO

LIBRARY OF CONGRESS CATALOG CARD NO. 67-18109

FIRST EDITION

Published simultaneously in Canada
by Little, Brown & Company (Canada) Limited

PRINTED IN THE UNITED STATES OF AMERICA

To
Virginia Geary Schendler
and
Leonard Baskin

Acknowledgments

THIS essay had its genesis in talks about Eakins with Leonard Baskin during my time in the Department of English at Smith College from 1956 to 1962. Originally intended for the Gehenna Press series Essays in Art, it was read, in earlier versions, by Baskin, and by his editor, Sidney Kaplan. Their criticisms were of great help to me, as were my frequent talks with Abram Lerner, Curator of the Joseph H. Hirshhorn Collection. I have been fortunate in having other good readers; the latest of them, Llewellyn Howland, has been among the most astute.

I have also been fortunate in coming to know people interested in Eakins and in his work: Seymour Adelman; Leon Arkus of the Carnegie Institute; Garnett McCoy of the Archives of American Art; Kneeland McNulty of the Philadelphia Museum; and Father Bartholomew Fair, President of the Catholic Historical Society of Philadelphia. Doris Palca and Mary Pollard Sullivan have been indispensable allies. Curators of public and private collections throughout the country and owners of individual works have been universally courteous and helpful, and I hope that this note will stand as recognition of my debt to them individually.

The main sources for the essay are Eakins' paintings; my failures must be measured against the paintings themselves, not against an impression supplied by a photograph, or against the views of another critic, and not against feelings about a painting at a distance. The main source of information about Thomas Eakins is Lloyd Goodrich's *Thomas Eakins, His Life and Work*, 1933. I have depended upon it. Margaret McHenry's *Thomas Eakins, Who Painted*, 1946, is largely the record of her talks with people who knew Eakins. Despite its peculiarities it is worth reading, and I have found it useful.

American art has been fortunate in its recent historians. Oliver Larkin,

Virgil Barker, E. P. Richardson, James Thomas Flexner, and Lewis Mumford are among those who have written histories of American art and books about artists which have been important to me. Looking back to the earlier years of the century, it is always good to find someone who values Eakins highly. I think of Sadakichi Hartmann, of Walter Pach, of Robert Henri. Recent commentary on Eakins' art has been uneven, but occasional articles such as those by Leslie Katz in 1956 and by James Fosburgh (about 1958) show that it is possible to respond sensitively to those qualities of his work that lie beneath the surface of representation.

An unpublished dissertation by Dorothy Ditter at the University of Pennsylvania was helpful in its attempt to define the cultural climate of Philadelphia during the 1876 Exhibition. Catalogs of collections of art later in the century add to the picture.

Fanny Herring's book on Gérôme has pictures of many of his paintings. Traubel's *With Walt Whitman in Camden* is the source of some of the information in the Whitman section. In *American Renaissance*, F. O. Matthiessen observed the spiritual kinship of Whitman and Eakins.

Charles Dickens, Henry James, Lincoln Steffens, Nathaniel Burt, Digby Baltzell, and George Biddle are among those whose commentaries on Philadelphia have been amusing and edifying. Helen Henderson's book on the Pennsylvania Academy is full of information. The autobiographies of Dr. Gross, John Sartain, Mrs. Gillespie, of Harrison Morris, McClure Hamilton, of F. H. Cushing, and biographies of Boies Penrose (who appears only peripherally, as it were, in Eakins' light: Samuel Murray did a sneering statue of him. Penrose is Eakins' antithesis, the man of immense native talent who believed in nothing but his own power); of Dr. Agnew, of Sloan and of Sheeler, are among the many that have helped to enlarge upon my impression of an era.

Philadelphia; New York; Goshen, New Hampshire, 1962-1966

Introduction

FACTS for a life of Eakins, which exist in no great abundance, are introduced throughout this essay and in the notes where they may seem more or less relevant to what he was painting or not painting at the time. His work, seemingly so objective, is closely connected with his personal life. But since what follows is a critical essay and not a biography, and since the venerable, inescapable, and essential data of a life, of birth and death, of comings and goings, of personal achievements and public failures have, for Eakins, no wide currency, some few of these are presented here, together with some others that may appear less essential, for their own sake, and so that we may know where we are going.

Thomas Eakins was born in Philadelphia on July 25, 1844. In 1846 his family moved to a large house at 1729 Mt. Vernon Street in Philadelphia, and this house was, except for brief periods, his home for the rest of his life. He graduated from Central High School in June 1861 with a B.A. degree, the equivalent of the American college degree today. He played no role in the Civil War.

In the autumn of 1866 he embarked for France, to study in Paris at the Ecole des Beaux Arts under Jean Leon Gérôme. (Samuel F. B. Morse, who had, years before, given up painting to make his fortune in another line of work, left at about the same time, for what was then called a triumphal tour of Europe.) What Eakins learned there was to affect his life as well as his painting. When he bought a copy of Rabelais in 1868 and wrote his father to praise the book trouble might have been predicted for him, for he meant to work in Philadelphia. He traveled with his father and with his sister Frances through France, Germany, Switzerland, and Italy in the summer of 1868. In November 1869 he left Paris for Spain and went to Madrid and then to Seville where he settled for a time. He did not visit Europe again after returning to Philadelphia in 1870.

His mother died in 1872. He had exhausted himself nursing her during the long months of her illness and painted little that year although he did complete an important portrait of his fiancée. His engagement to Katherine Crowell, which began in 1872, lasted until 1879 when she died at twenty-seven.

In 1875 he completed *The Gross Clinic*. This work, the most important by an American artist in the nineteenth century, was too strong a painting for Philadelphia and it was not hung in the Memorial Art Galleries of the Centennial Exhibition, for which Eakins had intended it.

The new building of the Pennsylvania Academy of Fine Arts at Broad and Cherry streets was opened on April 22, 1876, and that year Eakins assisted the ailing professor, Christian Schussele, in the painting classes. For the next few years he was in fact director of instruction at the Academy, though he was not named professor of drawing and painting until the summer of 1879, after the death of Schussele. In 1882 he became Director of the Art School at the Pennsylvania Academy but his position there was weakened when Edward Coates succeeded Fairman Rogers as Chairman of the School Committee in 1883.

On Christmas Eve, 1882, Margaret Eakins died. His favorite sister, she had been his companion skating and sailing; she had kept records of his paintings, and had been a strong encouraging force in his work. A year after her death, in January 1884, in his fortieth year, he married Susan Hannah Macdowell (daughter of William Macdowell, an engraver, individualist and spiritual descendant of Tom Paine). She had seen him first at a showing of *The Gross Clinic*. Later she was one of his best students at the Academy. They lived for about a year in what became Eakins' studio (it had been A. B. Frost's) at 1330 Chestnut Street, but Eakins returned to 1729 Mt. Vernon Street with his wife in 1885, possibly after his youngest sister, Caroline, married and left the Eakins home.

On February 13, 1886, Eakins was forced to resign his position at the Academy. The removal of the loincloth from a male model in one of the women's life classes, usually said to be the immediate cause of his dismissal, was only one of a number of affronts he had offered genteel sensibility in Philadelphia over the years. On February 22, some of his students, who had broken away from the Academy because of his resignation, formed the Art Students League with Eakins as their unpaid teacher. The school found various homes in the next six years — at 1429 Market, at 1338 Chestnut, at 18th and Market, and at 12th and Filbert streets — before it was disbanded in 1892. Samuel Murray, seventeen when he joined the school in the autumn of 1886, eventually became Eakins' closest friend. He was a substitute son for the rest of Eakins' life. He was in good part responsible for directing Eakins' attention to two important later subjects which found their forms in the boxing paintings and the portraits of Catholic clergymen.

In late July 1887, Eakins left Philadelphia for the B-T Ranch near Dickinson, North Dakota. (The Sioux had been driven from the open plains of Dakota only a few years before. Eakins painted no Indians, but the subject must have been in his mind. His later portrait of Frank Hamilton Cushing became, in my view, the most moving lament for the destruction of Indian civilization ever painted.) The B-T Ranch was owned, in part, by a good friend, Dr. Horatio Wood, Professor of Nervous Diseases at the University of Pennsylvania, and known, as Goodrich points out, for his work in therapeutics. Dr. Wood was later the subject of a fine full-length portrait by Eakins.

Eakins returned from Dakota in early October 1887, somewhat recovered from the fit of despondency that had hung over him since the debacle the year before. Later in the year he met Walt Whitman in Camden and began his portrait of the poet. In 1889 he painted the epic *Agnew Clinic*, a work which confirmed the critics and the public interested in these matters in their opinion that he was a butcher. His sister, Caroline Eakins Stephens, died in 1889.

Walt Whitman died in the spring of 1892. In May 1892, Eakins resigned from the Society of American Artists which had fallen in senescence in the dozen years since he had joined it. It had refused to hang *The Agnew Clinic*, among others of his works.

His niece, Ella Crowell, who had come to Philadelphia earlier in the decade to study, killed herself in 1897. (One of her still living cousins remembers hearing the blast of the shotgun at the Crowell farm in Avondale where Ella was kept locked in a room. Yet I recall hearing, at fourth hand, that Ella had killed herself in Eakins' studio. The second possibility, whether true or not, is typical of stories that attached themselves to him during and after his lifetime. I have heard, for instance, from a man who had known and photographed Eakins in his later years, that people in his neighborhood believed that the artist had strung up a corpse on the roof outside his studio for his *Crucifixion*. The model for that work was J. Laurie Wallace, a student of Eakins, who was alive half a century after the *Crucifixion* was painted.) Eakins' father, an extraordinary man, with whom he had lived for a lifetime on the closest and most friendly terms, died on December 30, 1899.

In 1896 he had his only one-man exhibition at Philadelphia's Earle Galleries. From 1899 to 1903 he served on the juries of the Carnegie Institute's International Exhibitions and he won medals before and after that time at numbers of other exhibitions. Among many artists there was a growing awareness of his achievement. But honors during his lifetime were less important to him than the rebuffs he had suffered. Though he had a wide circle of professional friends in Philadelphia, he felt himself isolated by the public's neglect of his work and alienated by the hostility of its taste makers. His work had become narrower in scope as he turned from what were, in effect, celebrations of large public and communal events and channeled all his energies into the most powerful and searching studies of individual human consciousness ever painted in this country.

His strong constitution and great strength failed him in the last years of his life, especially after 1910, and he became torpid, weak, unsteady, and nearly blind. He died at one o'clock in the morning on June 25, 1916. His death was remarked upon, appreciative essays were written in the newspapers, memorial exhibitions were held for him, but the nation as a whole, about to be drawn into the First World War, was no more conscious that its greatest painter had died than it had been aware of him while he lived.

When Susan Eakins died in 1938, twenty-one years after her husband, the collection of his work that had accumulated in their home since 1870 was dispersed. Many paintings were given to the Philadelphia Museum by Mrs. Eakins, but many others found their way into other collections, singly or in groups, and it is not possible today to arrive at a full estimate of Eakins' achievement by viewing the paintings at the Philadelphia Museum alone. Apart from the Philadelphia Museum, the largest single collection of Eakins' work, of preparatory sketches as well as of completed works, is that assembled by Joseph H. Hirshhorn and his astute curator, Abram Lerner. (When Eakins' sketches have been evaluated, new dimensions of his work will reveal themselves.) Stephen C. Clark, who may, one day, be acknowledged as this country's greatest collector (his taste was very nearly absolute, yet it developed), gave half a dozen works to the small but very impressive collection of Eakins at Yale. Smaller groups at the Metropolitan and at the Brooklyn Museum add to the picture. But *The Gross Clinic* hangs with two important portraits at Jefferson Medical School, *The Agnew Clinic* is at the University of Pennsylvania, many of the Catholic portraits are at St. Charles Seminary in Overbrook (where Father Bartholomew Fair has discovered or rescued more than one Eakins) while other individual pictures that add dimensions and depths to our understanding of what he was doing can be seen only if one has the leisure to seek them out in relatively obscure places throughout the country. The photographs in this volume, some never before published, others of pictures seldom seen by the public, illustrate the main flow of his work, but they imply an obligation, a necessity to discover the paintings themselves.

The works of most great artists are scattered; Eakins may indeed be more fortunate than many other masters, for large exhibitions of his paintings, like that of 1961-1962, are still possible. I think in these terms because there is something important to the nation in his vision of it, as well as in what he was . . . It is difficult to avoid the tones of exhortation.

Yet if we are not scientists alone (and I pretend to be neither aesthetician in the modern mode nor historian of art in the Germanic) and if we behave as if whatever is, or whatever happens, profoundly matters, then we may be moralists. To adopt the moral point of view is, in these matters as in others, to accept a limitation. It may be a limitation or even a failure of understanding that associates the development of a nation, the pretensions of a class, the decay of a city and the neglect of a great artist with one another. It may be that in approaching the artist's life through his art the meanings of both are distorted, or perhaps, in a larger sense, that in seeing his life as an *American* story (I hesitate to say tragedy), one's lights and shadows become too intense. And it may be at last, in what is, after all, a study of Eakins' art, that all these matters will seem irrelevant to some, including the oversimplified attempt to define both the possibilities for art and the defects of the genteel tradition through Emerson, who was no Philadelphian, and who could not have been produced by Philadelphia. Nevertheless, an immersion in Eakins' work and in the atmosphere of nineteenth-century Philadelphia produced the shape of this essay, together with whatever ideas may be discovered in it, and I believe they have their validity. If Philadelphia may appear to be the villain of the piece, it is no more so than the nation. I trust that no individual who considers himself related to the social class of nineteenth-century Philadelphians, and who is without the venial faults that I so generously attribute to them, will take personal offense.

The attempt to read other artists by Eakins' light may result in other kinds of distortions, and for these I must ask indulgence. My admiration for many of the American painters mentioned in this essay may find no direct expression in what I say about them. It is simply that Eakins puts them in the shade and that, in some cases, they cannot be seen as clearly there as they can in their own light. Surely the point of view adopted toward them is rigid and limited intellectually. It may be found, however, to yield its own kind of truth.

List of Illustrations

EAKINS

"I was born July 25, 1844. My Father's father was from the north of Ireland of the Scotch Irish. On my mother's side my blood is English and Hollandish. I was a pupil of Gérôme (also of Bonnat and of Dumont, sculptor). I have taught in life classes and lectured on anatomy continuously since 1873. I have painted many pictures and have done a little sculpture. For the public I believe my life is all in my work."

Yours truly,
Thomas Eakins
(1893)

(Eakins' autobiographical statement was written in 1893 in response to a request for information from the publisher of a biographical dictionary. It is quoted by Lloyd Goodrich in *Thomas Eakins, His Life and Work.*)

It is a handsome city, but distractingly regular . . . after walking about it for an hour or two . . . thoughts of making a large fortune by speculations in corn, came over me involuntarily. In connection with the Quaker Hospital, there is a picture by West. The subject is, our Saviour healing the sick and it is perhaps, as favorable a specimen of the Master as can be seen anywhere. Whether this be high or low praise, depends upon the reader's taste. In the same room, there is a very characteristic and life-like portrait by Mr. Sully, a distinguished American painter.

[Philadelphia] is more provincial than Boston or New York, and, there is, afloat in the fair city, an assumption of taste and criticism, savouring rather of those genteel discussions upon the same themes, in connection with Shakespeare and the Musical Glasses of which we read in the Vicar of Wakefield.

— Charles Dickens, *American Notes*, 1841

AT the city's center is the gray mass of City Hall. Two wide avenues meet there, both emerging from flat undistinguished cityscapes and that heavy pile interrupts them both. Enterprise along Broad and Market streets, to the north and east and west, has an air of accident and uncertainty about it, almost of apology for the high commercial intention which could produce at last only so much squalor. In the stolid baroque puzzle of the City Hall, where all views end, intention took another form. The people and their representatives wanted a suitable monument, massive, substantial, which would stand for the city, mark its pretensions and provide something for the builders and the officials. The building was begun in the 1870's, at the beginning, or perhaps in the middle, of one of the longest and most virile periods of sustained political corruption any American city has known. The tower erected above the City Hall, five hundred and ten feet of masonry, was meant to symbolize other kinds of aspiration. Alexander Calder's figure of William Penn stands atop it, thirty-seven feet high. He holds a scroll in one hand signifying peace, an order, an establishment, as Benjamin Franklin's image, everywhere in the city, signifies sagacity and probity, a devotion to the beauties of knowledge and to social betterment.

Until the center of the city was rebuilt in the middle of this century the Pennsylvania Railroad had run its tracks directly into Philadelphia on a great stone wall to Broad Street Station. Frank Furness had designed the station (opened in 1881, completed in 1894, demolished in 1952), in the Moorish-centennial style of his Pennsylvania Academy of Fine Arts. Earlier the railroad had laid out its acres of yards and tracks along the Schuylkill River below the place where Eakins painted his oarsmen in the 1870's. Before the end of the nineteenth century the railroad's Chinese Wall came to mark the division already established in the minds of proper Philadelphians between what was North and what was South of Market. *North of Market Street*, a novel of Philadelphia life now lost to posterity, tells of the difficulties of a couple who came to the city, took a house North of Market, and were shunned in consequence by the people they wished to know.

When Benjamin Eakins moved North of Market into the house at 1729 Mt. Vernon Street he had chosen a flourishing middle-class area of the city. That was in the mid-1840's. There were trees along the sidewalks, between the houses and in the back yards. The houses ran to four stories and they were not thrust meanly close to the street or to one another like the brick row dwellings builders were throwing up in other parts of Philadelphia in calculated imitation of English industrial slums.

There was a brick walk to the left of the Eakins house and a narrow strip of soil where in later years Susan Eakins grew flowers against the green board fence. Thomas Eakins painted his niece Ella there in 1876, a child at play with her toys. The back yard was partly bricked over, but there was ground for a garden. Gardens were kept behind all the homes, and in the summertime Eakins could look out upon the lush green geometry from the roof beneath his fourth floor studio.

That section of the city is a slum today. Windows are out of the red brick houses and doors of empty buildings are sealed off with sheets of galvanized iron. In the heat of August in 1964 the Negroes of this area rioted on Columbia Street and the apathy normal to the neighborhood momentarily gave way to the joys of looting.

Near what was the Eakins house, children now shout and play in the asphalt yard of the neighborhood school. On the corner is a *bodega* with works of art manufactured by General Foods. Across the street, the gray stone church, the SV. Lutherska Zionskyrkan (built in 1874, rebuilt in 1907), has become the Eglesia Adventista del Septimodia. The house, which Lloyd Goodrich (in the 1930's) found unchanged, its rooms still those that Eakins had lived in, was broken up into apartments after Susan Eakins died in 1938. Now the exterior shows signs of an accelerated decay. Green paint peels away around the windows and the dark tar paper covering the east wall on the fourth floor has rotted loose, showing the wide black boards beneath. The fence has been pushed down to the street and the brick walk is littered with bits of mid-twentieth-century America. The strip of earth bordering the walk is hard and bare. In the yard there are pieces of refrigerators and a scatter of broken glass. The barren gardens gather rubbish behind collapsing fences.

HENRY JAMES came to Philadelphia in the early part of this century for a brief amused visit. Through the mist of his circumlocutions he characterized the qualities of the city in decorously negative terms suited, in their way, to the city's temper. What struck that astute observer at first was its serenity, and the absence of any obstreperous or disturbing energy in its people. The secret of this serenity, he felt, lay in the fact that Philadelphia, beyond any other American city, was a society, settled and confirmed and content, and that having achieved the beatitude it had sought, it sought nothing else. Its imagination was at peace, and more, he remarked, it was determined to be at peace.

Behind the happy appearance lay the disconcerting reality of a city administration working in seeming independence of moribund society and "organized all for plunder and rapine, the gross satisfaction of official appetite, organized for eternal iniquity and impurity." Indifferent to this Infernal Machine, society, the determinedly happy family, "carried on the family business of buying and selling, of chattering and dancing"; the romantic in James conjured up the image of an *ancien régime* "dancing all consciously, on the thin crust of a volcano." Conditions were not as bad as that, or they were worse, for there was no revolution in the air. The failure of the ethical imagination was not confined to the upper classes. The sense of impotence in civic affairs afflicted the knowing and the ignorant on all levels of the social order. Political reform did not seem possible. At about the time of James's visit Lincoln Steffens found Philadelphia the least hopeful of American cities. The most powerful figure in the corrupt Republican party was Boies Penrose, whose antecedents had come to that place with William Penn;

but party bosses were drawn from all levels of the social order, and the masses were almost as corrupt if not as content as their masters. The intellectual and the moral vitality of the city derived from its professional class, which produced respectable men and first-rate talents in a number of fields. The archetype of fortune in the city was still, in a measure, old Benjamin Franklin, whose career might be used as an argument that effort might count for something honorable in history, that fame might conceivably be based upon some larger creativity than success in amassing wealth.

Benjamin Eakins came to Philadelphia in the third decade of the nineteenth century bent upon achieving a modest role in society. His father had been a craftsman, a weaver, and in choosing to become a writing master he meant to improve himself professionally and socially. He was a man of considerable strength and his decision to channel his energy into so narrow a profession implies a high degree of self-knowledge as well as a mature sense of reality. Restraint was always a strong element in his character, though he was not without imagination. He was an American who chose to achieve the good life through the mastery of his hand rather than the headlong pursuit of money or power. His imagination was largely reserved for his son for whom he conceived greater possibilities.

Benjamin Eakins believed in the social order for which he lettered congratulatory documents, its deeds, diplomas, certificates. This was in accord with the exercise of his profession in which doubt could have no place. Ornamental writing conformed to certain principles and was grounded in technique, not in individual vision; the handwriting master sought an ideal which both he and those who ordered his work could agree upon.

In American art, something like this same coincidence of vision and demand, or artist and patron, which the craftsman could still know in the mid-nineteenth century, had played its role in the work of John Singleton Copley. In Copley's Boston genius and conscience might still triumph when vision adjusted itself to what was demanded of it, when artist and sitter agreed that a pose drawn from the work of a fashionable English or Continental portraitist would precisely suit the present occasion. Though he might complain that Boston people had no interest in art beyond the speaking likeness, as a craftsman Copley sought to please, to produce the product expected of him, to paint character as if it were stable and unchanging, to paint the moment of social pretension as if it were forever. What life had done to his patrons, what they had not done, or what they had attempted and failed had no place in his splendid vision, for they had all triumphed in life, had all greatly succeeded. The triumph of character was certified by excluding the rude American world, the scene of triumph, and substituting for it an environment manufactured for the purpose, the dream world of elegant draperies and fine clothes, and an architecture of imagined grandeur marking unchanging time. In the main, the facts of American existence showed themselves not in landscape or in interior, but in the idea of character as something perfectly unambiguous, as fixed in an ordered world, a moral universe. If pre-Revolutionary America made Copley or his patrons uneasy, disquietude did not show itself in the rich and brilliant elegance of his work.

When Copley left Boston for London in 1775, Philadelphia became the creative focus of American art, and it was in Philadelphia, as E. P. Richardson has pointed out, "that painting passed out of the Colonial phase, beyond the efforts of a few scattered individuals, into that of a lively artistic life and professional organization. It was the home of Charles Willson Peale and his family, the organization of the first successful academy and annual exhibitions, the rise of still life, genre, and landscape, the center of the best engravers." Gilbert Stuart had come to Philadelphia in 1794 "to take a likeness of the President" and had lived there for ten years. [*See note, page 281.*] But Charles Willson Peale, no mere ornament to the city, was the vital force at the center of its art, healthily naïve in his enthusiasm for the American fact, and capable of achieving as much from the purely affirmative view of existence as Copley had, or as any artist has since.

When Peale died in 1825 leadership in the arts passed from Philadelphia, and a less vital principle than he had practiced came to dominate its art. Its most important artists, Sully, Inman, and Neagle were primarily portraitists who increasingly drew their manner from eighteenth-century English practice, from that of Lawrence and Raeburn and Hoppner, and their idea of elegance from the decorums and conventions of the genteel tradition. Inman hoped for "a higher and purer taste" to show itself; he meant that he wished to be released from the bondage to portraiture. The vitality of painting in Philadelphia, associated with Peale's interest in the world about him, drained away when money and social pretension came ever more directly to dictate the shape of its bland portrait art.

For the laymen who controlled the Pennsylvania Academy, art was a tool of genteel morality. Philip Hone, a New Yorker, had expressed their point of view when he observed that pictures were "the precious products of an art, the tendency of which is to refine the mind, enrich the imagination and soften the heart of man." No proper Philadelphian could have disagreed with him. George Caleb Bingham, who had studied at the Academy, found no audience there, for his base subjects were clearly not in the tradition of "high art." William Sidney Mount similarly erred in his failure to paint genteel subjects suitable to his talents. It is plain that the American tradition of concern for hard fact, which some historians see as distinguishing our art, was hardly its most striking feature in the first half of the nineteenth century. The tradition showed itself most strongly not in the yearly exhibitions at the Academy, but in popular art, and in popular lithographs and engravings.

In the year of Eakins' birth, Emerson published his essay "The Poet" among the *Essays Second Series*. There he attempted to establish the moral and intellectual bases for the self-reliance which would mark the coming poet's attempt to deal with American experience. The artist, Emerson wrote, would be the master of liberating symbols, a spokesman for universal nature and mind, and beyond that a more honest man than had come before, one more able to employ a tougher realism to deal with American facts, one capable of evoking great effects by his ability to see through appearance to deeper human realities. When he named the "rich poets," Emerson added Raphael's to the names of Homer, Chaucer and Shakespeare. Not surprisingly he found no one to equal them in nineteenth-century America.

"I look in vain for the poet whom I describe. We do not with sufficient plainness or sufficient profoundness address ourselves to life, nor dare we chaunt our own times and social circumstances. . . . We have as yet had no genius in America, with tyrannous eye, which knew the value of our incomparable materials, and saw in the barbarism and materialism of our times, another carnival of the same gods whose picture he so much admires in Homer: then in the Middle Age: then in Calvinism."

Though this may appear to require that a painter break entirely with a tradition systematically avoiding any deep immersion in experience, Emerson's idealism occasionally encouraged the opposite view. Poetry was concerned "to create an ideal world better than the world of experience," he wrote elsewhere, and the deeper insight of the poet could dispose "very easily of the most disagreeable facts." When he wrote, in "Self-Reliance," that the highest truth "shall exclude example and experience" his precept might as easily have encouraged the avoidance of the disagreeable as the expression of an audacity. For the arts, the possibilities marked by Emerson and the methods he appeared to foster brought Walt Whitman to a boil, but they might also have given heart to Mrs. Sigourney, the "Sweet Singer of Hartford." As a representative man of the highest order, Emerson embodied in his thought that deep split in American thinking, grounded in the genteel tradition, which valued experience in practical affairs, but insisted that the rule of the artist was to build ideal worlds.

On the whole optimistic about the artist's chances in America, he was relatively certain that the chosen would be rewarded in the here and now. "Money," he wrote, "is in effects and laws, as beautiful as roses. Property keeps the accounts of the world and is always moral. The property will be found where the labor, the wisdom and the virtue have been in nations, in classes, and (the whole lifetime considered, with the compensations) in the individual also." [*See note, page 281.*] This happy banality had something of a corollary in his reflection that the poet "is isolated among his contemporaries by his truth and by his art, but with this consolation in his pursuits, that they will draw all men sooner or later. For the experience of each age requires a new confession, and the world seems always waiting for its poet."

Emerson meant to encourage honesty in the arts by his rhetoric; he could relinquish his certainty that merit would find its reward in this world only by substituting for it the romantic image of the artist as martyr: "Artists must be sacrificed to their art. Like bees, they must put their lives into the sting they give. What is a man good for without enthusiasm? And what is enthusiasm but the daring of ruin for its object?"

Strangely or not, it appears that Eakins' faith in his art was grounded in the same sort of idealism that moved Emerson. He began his career certain that honesty and attention to his craft would be rewarded by an audience equal to his art. But he was also to exhibit the "dare-devil, dare-god originality" that Emerson found in Rabelais and hoped for in young Americans, that strong streak of antiauthoritarianism that would undercut the decorums of his time and place simply by remaining true to his perceptions and to his experience.

HENRY JAMES, born a year earlier than Eakins, was another of the generation for which Emerson had so much hope. Writing of Emerson, James discovered his "great distinction and his special sign" in the fact that he had a more vivid conception of the moral life than anyone else in his genius for "seeing character as a real and supreme thing." "No one has had so steady and constant . . . a vision of what we require and what we are capable of in the way of aspiration and independence. With Emerson it is ever the capacity for moral experience." "We have the impression," James wrote, "that life had never bribed him to look at anything but the soul."

No one was of course more concerned with the moral life than James himself, yet there was a large difference between his practice and Emerson's. James took it as "a sign of Emerson's singular power, that he is a striking exception to the general rule that writings live in the last resort by their form." He was also struck by Emerson's insensitivity to whole areas of literature. Walking with him through the galleries of the Louvre and of the Vatican, he remarked chords in the great man that "did not vibrate," or "were wholly absent." Struck with "the anomaly of a man so refined and intelligent being so little spoken to by works of art," James may have felt it unnecessary to remark that in his deficiency Emerson was a representative American. The Emerson who could feel that Hawthorne's novels "were not worthy of him," might have been similarly unresponsive to the human meanings Eakins was to discover in his art.

The incapacities of his audience, their lack of concern with form, their hostility to the deeply serious had concerned James in more than one story. In "The Author of Beltraffio" Mark Ambient describes his wife as "a very nice woman, extraordinarily well-behaved, upright and clever with a tremendous lot of good sense about a good many matters. Yet her conception of a novel . . . is a thing so false that it makes me blush. It's a thing so hollow, so dishonest, so lying, in which life is so blinked and blinded, so dodged and disfigured, that it makes my ears burn. It's two different ways of looking at the whole affair. . . . And they're irreconcilable. . . . If you're going into this kind of thing," he advises the narrator, "there's a fact you should know beforehand; it may save you some disappointment. There's a hatred of art, there's a hatred of literature — I mean of the genuine kinds. Oh the shams — those they'll swallow by the bucket."

The young narrator discovers the "signs of a sober fanaticism" in Mrs. Ambient, in "her air of incorruptible conformity, her tapering monosyllabic correctness [which] began to affect me as in themselves a cold thin flame. Certainly, at first, she resembled a woman with as few passions as possible; but if she had a passion at all it would indeed be that of Philistinism." In Mrs. Ambient, James produced the embodiment of the "attractive" civilization which the artist discovers both hostile to his art and humanly destructive. [*See note, page 281.*]

James's consciousness fitted him for membership in Emerson's great audience, whatever his own genteel incapacities. The young James who had been shocked by Turgenev's coming to the door in his dressing gown might, it is true, have suffered even more grossly before the heavy-gutted figure of the later Eakins in an undershirt prepared to do the portrait of a Philadelphia lady. Yet as there is much in Emerson's, there is much in James's intelligence and in his taste that calls directly for the kind of art Eakins was to shape. James admired Copley, but found lacking in him the quality that distinguishes so much of Eakins' best work: "As for suggestiveness, he rendered perfectly and exhaustively all that he saw, and he saw nothing that he could not render. He was definite, as we say; but that adventurous vision of the indefinite which has brushed with its wing all the very greatest works of art is never reflected here." Nearly twenty years later, in 1893, James qualified his great admiration for Sargent in the same way: "The gift that he possesses he possesses completely — the immediate perception of the ends and of the means." But there were deeper necessities:

> Putting aside the question of the subject . . . the highest result is achieved when to this element of quick perception a certain faculty of brooding reflection is added. I use this name for want of a better, and I mean the quality in the light of which the artist sees deep into his subject, undergoes it, absorbs it, discovers in it new things that were not on the surface, becomes patient with it, and almost reverent, and in short, enlarges and humanizes the technical problem.

If he knew of an American artist who filled that prescription, James did not speak of him.

Sargent did know Eakins, and the two men respected one another. At the beginning of this century, near the end of Eakins' career, Sargent was asked by his hostess whom he would like to see during his stay in Philadelphia. "There is Eakins for instance," he replied. "Who is Eakins?" his hostess is supposed to have asked. Sargent had been audacious in speaking that name. Eakins did not move in the Philadelphia society frequented by Sargent. There may appear something unlikely about the story, since Eakins had once achieved a certain notoriety in his city. Yet that had been forgotten, and the story as myth bespeaks the truth of Eakins' neglect.

Having chosen to leave the country where society was "too sparse for synthesis," James returned in the early part of the twentieth century in part to observe the American scene. He visited a great art collection in Philadelphia and recorded his impression of a place where "appetite had broken out and was feeding itself to satiety." He took the collection, probably either

John G. Johnson's of Italian and Flemish art or Peter A. B. Widener's more eclectic one (which ranged from Raphael, Rembrandt, Velasquez and El Greco, through Gainsborough, Hoppner, Lawrence and Romney, to Degas and Whistler), as a demonstration of the fruits of the acquisitive instinct, feeling himself "catch in the very act, one of the great ingurgitations of the hungry machine." He saw it as the exhibition of a "case," and made less allowance for the character and taste of the Philadelphia lawyer or of the Philadelphia financier than he might have. That is understandable. If he saw Johnson's collection there would have been no reason to distinguish the single work of Eakins which Johnson had acquired. No one except Eakins collected Eakins, and Henry James may not have known his name. [*See note, page 282.*]

EAKINS graduated from Central High School in 1861 in the top quarter of his class. The school was known for its high scholastic standards and for the strength of its curriculum in the sciences. The strong feeling for languages and for science, especially for mathematics, that he developed there never left him. He developed no enthusiasm for literature, and his training in art achieved its highest expression in perspective drawings of machinery *(Figure 1)*.

He was old enough to have fought in the Civil War but he did not enlist. He was his father's only son, and Benjamin Eakins may have asked him not to join the Union Army. The decision was a natural one considering the family's politics, but it was probably also grounded in Quaker principle. Philadelphia was more nearly a Southern than a Northern city, and the Eakinses were Democrats, the party of Pierce and Buchanan, of accommodation and compromise with the South. Philadelphia's Democrats considered Lincoln and the Republicans dangerous radicals. Certainly no idea of moral crusade attached to the war; Philadelphians did not think of it as meant to bring about the emancipation of the Negro.

Relatively little is known of that period of his life. He studied anatomy at Jefferson Medical College, drew from the antique and attended life classes (the models were, in all probability, decently clothed) at the Pennsylvania Academy, and assisted his father in lettering documents and teaching ornamental writing. In 1866 he and his father decided that he should go to Paris for further training in art. He had considered becoming a doctor, but now had made his choice of vocation, solemnizing it by what was, for that time, that city, and that closely knit family, as radical a plan as the decision to stay out of the war. It was an important decision for him as an artist, for

1. PERSPECTIVE OF A LATHE
1860. 22 x 16¼. Joseph H. Hirshhorn Collection.

during his three years in Europe he built the groundwork for a style that could not have been developed in Philadelphia.

In Paris in the autumn of 1866 he enrolled in the class of Jean Leon Gérôme, the most respected master at the Ecole des Beaux Arts. It is difficult not to believe, in retrospect, that Gérôme might have destroyed him as an artist had Eakins been merely a first-rate talent. A reasonable admirer of Eakins' work has said that Gérôme had no effect upon his development at all, yet the fact is that he was demonstrably influenced, however much he turned away from his master to methods and to a style more expressive of his own vision. [*See note, page 282.*]

Eakins, during his later years, always spoke well of Gérôme, his fidelity surviving the discovery of the teacher's inadequacies. When he also recommended Gérôme's work as painter and sculptor, one feels it was more the voice of the filial journeyman than the judgment of a peer. It was also the response of a man who, after all, saw his master from the distance of nineteenth-century Philadelphia, a disadvantaged position from which Gérôme must have appeared the very embodiment of the great traditions of Western Art. But it was more than that. The two men had temperamental affinities and similar views of the aims and significance of art, quite apart from their differing practices; strangely, it was Gérôme who, in his fashion, prepared the way for Eakins' discovery of Velasquez.

It would be pleasant if one could rehabilitate Gérôme's reputation as a painter so that Eakins' recommendation of him might become more meaningful. But it would be a difficult and a questionable labor at best, requiring the devotion of a fanatic and a catholic taste of heroic proportions. Gérôme painted as he taught, insisting upon precise draftsmanship, precisely engineered perspective, upon composition and balance and contrast, upon what he conceived to be the science of art given individual expressive form by his own personality. Yet there was something lacking in his nature, something that contrived banal plots for his anecdotal imaginings; and technique, vision, intellect, his nervous system in all its parts all contributed to the final impossible effect. Though he warned in his teaching of the dangers of the picturesque he was himself addicted to it. His imagination typically chose its subjects from the exotic Near East, from lush moments in history, or from myth. Henry James was struck by the hardness of his work, the effect of his technique, but more, by its banality.

It is not surprising, therefore, that Gérôme was fully appreciated in his time. The Duc de Guermantes, whose opinion Proust did not value, thought highly of him. *The Duel After the Masquerade* (at the Walters Art Gallery in Baltimore) was once a very famous picture; and *L'Eminence Grise* (at the Boston Museum of Fine Arts) was equally well known. J. Alden Weir called that painting "one of Gérôme's greatest pictures," and William de Leftwich Dodge, a Philadelphian, thought it "one of the best composed pictures I know of." *Pygmalion and Galatea* (at the Metropolitan) was considered a daring work. These paintings survive as historical curiosities today; yet it must be said that they may occasionally have a certain uncanny quality that is beyond mere illustration. [*See note, page 283.*]

The subjects illustrated by the engravings of his works may not appear to invite further inquiry. In *The Poet's Dream* naked maidens, seen through a mist but splendidly displayed on a beach, are observed by the poet and his muse, both properly dressed. In *The Rose* a buxom maiden tosses a rose from the stone balcony of her keep to the gaily caparisoned horseman below. *Love the Conqueror* is a haloed cupid in a den of purring lions, tigers, and panthers. In these and in other works it is as if Gérôme were aiming at surreal effects through his perspective and through the hardness of his line. But the intense efforts underlying them may provide nothing more than a sadly definitive example of defeat of the will by a quality of mind which will not support it.

Sargent, it is said, never doubted the rightness of the methods he was being taught by Carolus-Duran in Paris. Significantly, Eakins began to assert very personal qualities at an early point in his studies. He "was in the dumps" he wrote his father in November 1867, for he had made a drawing on his canvas "according to Gérôme's directions . . . then he said not bad, that will do, now I will mix your colors which you will put on." He came to resent Gérôme's tampering with his work in any way, and after he left Paris he wrote his father that Gérôme "aside from overthrowing completely the ideas I had got before at home . . . has never been able to assist me much, and often bothered me by mistaking my troubles."

Yet he remained loyal to this master, who had, in his own way, provided the basis for the kind of understanding necessary to any Philadelphian who hoped to paint the figure with some authority. Earlier, he had resented the emphasis upon the antique at the Pennsylvania Academy where students were still led to correct their life studies by reference to casts. The profoundly liberating shift of emphasis to the nude model at the Ecole des Beaux Arts was undoubtedly the most important thing that happened to him there. Eakins had a Philadelphian's suspicion of the nude at first, but through

Gérôme came to believe that a naked man or woman might legitimately be the subject for a painting.

In his teaching Gérôme did not completely do away with the study of classical sculpture, but he made forceful distinctions between one "antique" era and another, making plain his preference for the work of Phidias and his predecessors to the work of the "Greek decadence" which was, he observed, "the course of David back to the antique." The *Apollo Belvedere* and *Diana the Huntress* led David to the *Rape of the Sabines* and *Leonidas at Thermopylae*, works, he felt, which were "cold, without character and without life." When he wrote that "young artists should be nourished with the marrow of lions, and led to the purest springs to quench their thirst," he was implying aesthetic distinctions never made at the Pennsylvania Academy, and a view of the artist that could only have disturbed its trustees. Rhetoric of that sort was not heard in Philadelphia.

The sacred passion, so well disguised in his own work, emerged in his teaching. He warned against that kind of naturalism, that kind of undiscriminating realism, which was the death of so much nineteenth-century painting. Pictures had to display perfect plastic control, certainly; they had also to portray "ideas simply comprehended and clearly, powerfully expressed." This might disastrously move students to pursue an art very like his own, but only weak-minded students. He believed in a student's thinking his way into a subject in a manner that would reveal his own quality of mind, whatever it was. "You are not thinking of the matter in hand," he would tell a pupil. "You have in mind some picture that you have seen somewhere." He would not permit "eccentricity." His students might not depart from the strong and the reasonable. But reason and observation were given life by the artist's passion, and art had to appeal to the heart and the soul by way of that passion. Fidelity to nature was the unquestioned necessity, but "Imitation must serve expression," he warned, "or you will remain children."

Gérôme's students knew him as a man of actively masculine disposition; he was a laconic person, severe in his judgments, grave, dignified, reserved. Eakins responded to the man if he questioned his teaching, and he appears to have modeled much of his own teaching upon what he had learned directly or indirectly from him. He would tell his students to avoid exaggeration, yet like Gérôme he sought to encourage any expression of strong individuality, of expressive force in their work and would urge them to "go to the full extent of things" in the attempt to lay bare whatever truth moved them.

The technique Gérôme taught, the insistence upon strong drawing and the exact placement of objects in space may not seem to contain the seeds of liberation for any art, yet it appealed to that strong element in Eakins' nature, revealed early enough in the perspective sketches of machinery drawn in high school, his concern with fact, his devotion to science. And although he rejected the carefully filled in drawing as the basis for his teaching or for his art, something very much like it became the technical basis for some of his most important early work, his rowing scenes, his watercolors, and some of his genre work.

"A teacher can do very little for his pupil and should only be thankful if he don't hinder him, and the greater the master mostly the less he can say," he wrote his father. He left Paris as soon as he felt he could teach himself no more there, and after a session in the Prado he wrote in his notebook "*Il faut me décider de ne jamais peindre de la façon du patron. . . . Il est loin de peindre comme les Ribera et les Velasquez, quoiqu'il soit aussi fort qu'aucun frotteur.*" If Gérôme was only a technician at last, a *frotteur*, a scumbler laying down his opaque colors between the lines of meticulous drawings, something in his way of seeing was to carry over into his greatest student's work, there to be infinitely transformed. [*See note, page 283.*]

THE transformation took place in Spain in 1869 and '70 where Eakins discovered Velásquez and the possibility of other kinds of understanding. The antithesis of Gérôme as a painter, Velásquez was nevertheless another man to whose character he could respond, and now, luckily, that character was revealed clearly in his work. The reserve, the dignity were there, the solidity and the strong sense of reason showing themselves in the absence of distortion and exaggeration and in the rejection of violence to achieve effect.

Given what he was, Eakins could see in Rubens, on the other hand, only a monster concerned with display. He wrote to his father from Madrid on December 2, 1869:

. . . I left Paris Monday night in a pouring rain of course. All my friends came to see me. If it had not been winter time and if I had not known and feared the Atlantic voyage, not being well, I would have come home straight, but since I am now here in Madrid I do not regret at all my coming. I have seen big painting here. When I had looked at all the paintings by all the masters I had known I could not help saying to myself all the time, it's very pretty but it's not all yet. It ought to be better, but now I have seen what I always thought ought to have been done and what did not seem to me impossible. O what a satisfaction it gave me to see the good Spanish work so good so strong so reasonable so free from every affectation. It stands out like nature itself. And I am glad to see the Rubens things that is the best he ever painted and to have them alongside the Spanish work. I always hated his nasty vulgar work and now I have seen the best he ever did I can hate him too. The best picture he ever made stands by a Velásquez. His best quality that of light on flesh is knocked by Velásquez and that is Rubens' only quality while it is but the beginning of Velásquez's. Rubens is the nastiest most vulgar noisy painter that ever lived. His men are twisted to pieces. His modelling is always crooked and dropsical and no marking is ever in its right place or anything like what he sees in nature, his people never have bones, his color is dashing and flashy, his people must all be in the most violent action, must use the strength of Hercules if a little watch is to be wound up, the wind must be blowing great guns even in a chamber or dining room, everything must be making a noise and tumbling about there must be monsters too for his men were not monstrous enough for him. His pictures always put me in mind of chamber pots and I would not be sorry if they were all burnt.

The violent reaction was in part the Philadelphian's, but it had other meanings. For Gérôme's work, at another pole from Rubens' in most ways, also lacked the qualities of "big painting" as Eakins conceived it — the consistent searching of character, the fusion of significant matter and spirit in bodies that had weight, the evoked sense of an intelligence in meaningful connection with its world. Beyond these, organizing, including, and indistinguishable from them at last, was the effect of a work; what made for the effect was the kind of beauty the artist habitually sought. In the work of Velásquez Eakins felt that he had discovered his own necessity for the first time, the attempt to achieve "*la délicatesse et la force en même temps.*"

The names of Velásquez, Rembrandt and Ribera reappear in his notes, touchstones of his quest: he was looking for an expression of energy joined to insight. It was a quest for ultimate meaning and intelligence rather than for technique. And so there was to be no direct line from any of these painters to his own work. If he were to achieve, in Goodrich's phrase, the "distinction and grave splendor" of Velásquez, the force of Ribera, the penetration of Rembrandt, these would discover themselves in forms of their own, through new ways of honesty and new uses of the imagination.

In Spain in the spring of 1870 he completed his first picture, *A Street Scene in Seville (Figure 2)*, a large canvas showing a musical troupe of street dancers, a family of three, a young father, mother, and daughter performing before a wall in sunlight and shadow. In some respects it was a conventional French genre composition, yet a quality distinguished it, a feeling for light and for time, for mortal life suspended in a transient moment. It was good work, but he required subjects closer to home, to speak his own language.

2. A STREET SCENE IN SEVILLE
1870. 63 x 42½. Mrs. John R. Garrett, Sr.

3

EAKINS returned from Europe in 1870. Whatever possibilities were open to him as a man and as an artist in the Philadelphia of that period, he chose to live at home and to begin by painting his family, instinctively discovering beauty where a Rembrandt or a Vermeer might have sought it. He moved outward from his family to their intimate friends for subjects, then to his friends sailing and hunting in the waterways, the marshes and fields of New Jersey and Pennsylvania. No other American artist has ever begun his life's work with more quiet unassertive certainty, with more mature mastery of atmosphere and effect.

His early work communicates his loving acceptance of everything he sees, his youthful consciousness of time, of mortality, of an era passing — communicates it with an attention to fact, certainty, but with a lyricism and even a romanticism one does not generally associate with his name in histories of American art. In this work the facts of Eakins' painting are never felt apart from the heat with which he painted them, and the sense of restrained emotion underlying the fact always distinguishes it.

How an audience of his time might respond to this heat is another matter. It was unaccustomed to seeing beauty where he looked for it. There were aspects of his work before *The Gross Clinic* which Philadelphians might have found aesthetically unappealing or offensive. In the celebration of his subjects, in his choice and treatment of the beautiful, Eakins gave shape and force to a vision to which they were entirely unaccustomed. He discovered the hidden and charged vitality of the ordinary, simultaneously implying its significance and consciously understating his perceptions.

One must not obscure the basis for the deep appeal of his art by correcting the opinion of an earlier time, which found his work harsh, brutal and unseemly, through recourse to that apparently harmless, critical reflex, the observation that he was a realist of uncompromising honesty and integrity. He was that, to be sure, but it is more important for our time to see that his objectivity is not to be felt apart from his quest for beauty, or from the emotional force with which he communicated his perceptions. What moves us in his great work is the emotionally perceived identity of his world and not its objective identity. [*See note, page 283.*]

"To the beautiful," George Caleb Bingham wrote in the last year of his life, eight years after Eakins had begun to paint in Philadelphia, "belongs endless variety." Beauty was to be found in what the great artist saw as beautiful, and not only in a classical ideal of "symmetry and elegance of form." Bingham might have found beauty, as Eakins himself had, in the early portraits of his sister Frances *(Figure 3)* and of Frances and Margaret, *At the Piano (Figure 4)*, both done in 1870 or 1871, where subservience to a classical or modish ideal had no part in the artist's vision.

The honesty of these portraits is undeniably one of their most striking characteristics. No formula transforms Frances' irregular profile or Margaret's flat, broad face into more conventionally beautiful features. Nor are their poses contrived to discover ordinary beauties of form. But honesty is alloyed with other no less important qualities, an instinctive intellectual concern with the significance of a pose, an ability to communicate, especially in the second picture, a mood in which the artist himself participates, and a sense of design whose stabilities and disequilibriums imply both restraint and movement, a design suggestive of the kind of smoldering life we sense in Margaret's face.

These portraits were beginnings. When he posed Margaret and Caroline in the 1870 or 1871 *Home Scene (Figure 5)*, he discovered other tensions in that suspended moment, and his vision of the real was charged with symbolic meanings. Margaret carries the burden of his feeling as she turns away from those sheets of music where sound, time, and light suspend themselves, and twists into the light to watch Caroline toying with her slate. With one of her hands she plays with the kitten on her shoulder; she rests her head on the other. Both girls support their bodies and prop their heads with elbows and hands. Posture and gesture play off against one another, the latent force of awareness in Margaret's leaning figure set against the suspended reverie of the child on the floor. Eakins' role is almost palpable as he creates from these subtle oppositions that atmosphere of quiet yet intense awareness that concentrates at last in Margaret's face. Through her protective yet detached presence he says something about the necessities of destiny, of character and fate formed and forming in this world.

Margaret was Eakins' favorite sister; his instinct was that neither love nor feeling could be expressed through an idealization that might rob Margaret of her identity, and, in 1871, he painted her as a swarthy broad-featured girl in a corduroy jacket and dark hat in *Margaret in Skating Costume (Figure 6)*, a girl whose warmth and vitality are suspended once more in a moment of abstraction. In an oil sketch of the same year Margaret *(Figure 7)* is seen full face, the light on the right side of her face, again not conventionally beautiful but clearly felt as beautiful by her brother. She is profoundly alive sensuously, the deep reserve of her own feeling showing itself through eyes now fully open, observing the spectator. [*See note, page 284.*]

In 1872 Eakins painted a large full-length portrait of Katherine Crowell *(Figure 8)*, a girl to whom he was to remain engaged for the next seven years. The size of the painting and its use of greatly increased interior light are signs of a change of mood and a growth in self-assurance. Katherine, wearing a light summer dress, is seated with an open fan in her right hand, her left hand open playfully above the kitten in her lap. Though she has a certain fragile grace, her features are undistinguished. Pose, carriage, and gesture may suggest a sweetness and a gentleness but the absence of any distinctive vitality in that body. How can a reading of this sort account for the immediate effect of great lyrical strength and beauty that the portrait so unmistakably produces? Eakins' honesty saves it, one is inclined to say, from becoming sentimental or banal. But it is more than a matter of treatment. In *Katherine* a quality of mind reveals itself in color and form through a technique of which it is absolute master, through a draftsmanship and a style inseparable from the evoked feeling.

The warmth of the painting is arresting, its subdued richnesses of light and color surprising us in that dark room, with its golds, mahogany reds, and golden browns. The warm morning light floods from the left and makes luminous the right side of the painting. Sunlight glances obliquely from the dark mahogany of the paneling and from the dark leaded glass behind Katherine. The partially illuminated Victorian interior is substantial, dark, massive, and the high upholstered chair with its knobs and turnings, its ornate back and red plush covering, is a presence. Here are the symbols of an era and of an entire moral order. The solidities and darknesses of that room do

3. FRANCES EAKINS
1870 or 1871. 24 x 20. Nelson Gallery, Atkins Museum (Nelson Fund), Kansas City, Missouri.

4. AT THE PIANO (FRANCES AND MARGARET EAKINS)
1870 or 1871. 22 x 18. Permanent Collection of the University Art Museum, University of Texas (Gift of Dr. Caroline Crowell).

5. HOME SCENE
1870 or 1871. 21¾ x 18. The Brooklyn Museum.

not oppress Katherine but she *is* dominated by them. They are emblems of the society that formed her character and tamed her personality. It is not a harshly realized truth; gentleness and honesty lie at the core of the painting's effect — that quiet tension of delicacy and power grounded in the intellectual depth and emotional soundness which were to inform all Eakins' great work.

Three years later, during the early months of 1875, Eakins painted Katherine's sister Elizabeth *(Figure 9)*. It was a larger portrait beneath the surface of whose classic restraint one may be conscious of personal tensions and even of passions more acutely felt. The handling of light and dark is more dramatic, and their control at once more severe and more romantic. Elizabeth, in a dark dress and hat, straight-backed and intent, is seated at the piano, her body emerging from and dominating a background nearly black at the left, bluish gray at the upper right. Light touches her neck and part of her face; it falls upon the music, the thumb of her left hand, the edge of her right. There is a grand subdued elegance in this vision, a vivacity and an intensity in pose, gesture, and posture that is very unlike Katherine's dreamy lassitude. It is said that Eakins preferred Elizabeth to Katherine, and it is not difficult to understand why. Elizabeth is more woman than she is childlike creature of a civilization; she is as fully alive sensuously beneath her dark dress as Margaret was in the earlier sketch, her sexuality quite as forcefully, if more obliquely, projected. Through the strong romantic forces working within it, through the use of shadow and of bold yet subtle contrasts of light and dark, the current of Eakins' early realism is made richer, more mysterious, more compelling emotionally. Responding to Elizabeth's loveliness, Eakins subtly discovers the vitality that animated it. The girl dominates the dark room, seemingly unconscious of herself in the fading light. The portrait of her shows Eakins' power as he had not revealed it before. He told his wife, years later, that he was "satisfied" with it, and kept it over the mantel in his living room.

Benjamin Howard Rand (1874) *(Figure 10)* was the first of Eakins' portraits of scientists, and another in which his genius, taking its roots in a greater tradition, bypassed the moribund habits of official late nineteenth-century portraiture. Professor Rand, a spectacled, bearded man seated behind his desk, strokes a cat with his left hand and points to a page of a book with his right. This relaxed gravely amused way of seeing the professional man is as quietly surprising as the color emerging from so dark a painting. The professor is not stiffened in a stereotyped pose; he looks down as he leans

6. MARGARET IN SKATING COSTUME
1871. 24 x 20½. Collection of the Philadelphia Museum of Art.

7. MARGARET (STUDY)
1871. 19¼ x 16. Joseph H. Hirshhorn Collection.

8. KATHERINE
1872. 61½ x 50. Yale University Art Gallery, bequest of Stephen C. Clark.

9. ELIZABETH AT THE PIANO

1875. 72 x 48. Addison Gallery of American Art, Phillips Academy, Andover, Mass.

10. BENJAMIN HOWARD RAND
1874. 60 x 48. Jefferson Medical College, Philadelphia.

over his cluttered desk. The objects in the room and on the desk — the test tube full of a red liquid, the brass microscope, the pink rose and green leaves lying on the book, the blue paper hanging over the desk's edge, the rose-colored drape thrown over a chair — reflect elements of the scientist's personality, a controlled disorder, a restrained sybaritism, a sense of humor. The effect of *Benjamin Rand* may be less unified than the lyricism of *Katherine (Figure 8)* or the romantic force of *Elizabeth at the Piano (Figure 9);* it has nevertheless its own quality, a largeness of feeling, a beauty and a richness reminiscent of the great traditions of Dutch and Flemish portraiture. It has nothing to do with the painterly elegance of eighteenth-century English practice as refined and attenuated by Sully and Neagle.

It is the communicated depth of feeling that gives life to the extraordinary series of sculling scenes Eakins painted at this time. Among the great interests of this early work is the felt quest for delicacy and force and the immediate emergence of a personal vision pursued now with the broader more painterly style of the early portraits, now with a tighter more linear control suggestive of Gérôme. The method of the perspective sketches for the rowing scenes is a direct inheritance from Gérôme, however much the force of the paintings themselves derives from his own temperament.

In general the sculling scenes are painted with something like the technique of Gérôme, the technique of the near view, their objects carefully defined, their compositions based upon mathematically conceived perspective drawings. But the self-imposed restraints of technique, together with the characteristic ones, of mood, of gesture, of composition, are once again inextricable from the most deeply grounded feelings for time and place.

These scenes were set on the Schuylkill flowing through Fairmount Park, still one of the most beautiful city parks in America. Eakins was an accomplished oarsman, and the delight he took in rowing, in the river, and in the park found expression in that early masterpiece, painted in 1871, *Max Schmitt in a Single Scull (Figure 11).* Though most Americans still do not know Eakins' name, many who know paintings remember this haunting work. Max Schmitt, holding both oars in his left hand, his right hand at rest on his knee, turns to look at us. The glance is immediate, and the man lives. Time between him and the spectator is less than the few feet of water, the few inches of canvas separating the scull *Josie* from the frame's edge. The painting is not in the mood of Whitman's "Crossing Brooklyn Ferry," but its theme is strongly

11. MAX SCHMITT IN A SINGLE SCULL
1871. 32¼ x 46¼. The Metropolitan Museum of Art, Alfred N. Punnett Fund
and Gift of George D. Pratt, 1934.

reminiscent of Whitman's identification of the poet with the spectator a century or centuries distant.

The Schuylkill mirrors the autumn afternoon; the late sunlight catches Schmitt in his scull, the bridge over the river, the cloud above, and the artist himself, in his earliest self-portrait, pulling at his oars in the middle distance. The bridge laces and arches from the shadows of the foliage on the left to the shadows of the bank on the right where the water is darker. Eakins' profoundly emotional response to light (remembered and recaptured in his studio) envelops other themes.

This is a melancholy painting, asserting the impossible contraries of existence in time. The warm moment is suspended in time, yet flowing, passing. The October sunlight exists forever, caught there, and is long gone. The bridge is an assertion of connection in time, as Eakins, in the robust health of his late twenties, facing us as he moves away, transcends it, includes it. Virgil Barker writes, "It is one of those hours, when nature itself prolongs the light into a promise of timelessness, and gives the most analytical eye opportunity to discern the deep transparencies and subtle solidities which spiritualize the world of matter." Max Schmitt looks at us out of his mortality, and out of the astonishing light of that painting.

The theme of time and mortality runs through most of Eakins' work. In the earlier paintings it takes its meaning in part from this quiet, unobtrusive symbolism. Though the emphasis of the later work may shift to a more intense reading and penetration of individual psychology, the theme and the symbolic habit will simply take on new forms. Early or late a subtlety in the treatment of theme and in the expression of force, an aesthetic sophistication of the highest order, distinguishes a vision that is as emotionally moving as it is humanly profound.

Time and light were plainly the significant themes of *The Pair-Oared Shell* (1872) *(Figure 12)*. The mathematically precise perspective drawing gives no hint of the painting's effect, of the massive downthrust of the bridge, the counterthrust of landscape behind, and of the men, moving like apparitions yet still at the crux of the cross formed by land and column. A late afternoon light barely touches the heads, arms, and legs of Barney and John Biglen and colors the massive stone column of the old Columbia Bridge as they pull out of its deep shadow, but not into light. The mood is set by the browns of the river, the grays of the shore, and by Eakins' very personal yet classical use of the symbolism of arrested movement. Caught here against the monumental form of the stone pier — the permanence of stone set in

12. THE PAIR-OARED SHELL
1872. 24 x 36. Collection of the Philadelphia Museum of Art.

flowing water, touched by changing light, the great blocks of stone themselves eroding — the rowers, suspended in time, are time's creatures. The light fades and the river flows darkly. Immersed in this moment, the brothers are serious, stoical. Yet the painting has meanings beyond its statement of themes for it is an assertion of human strength and dignity transcending mortality and the erosions of time. Whereas Max Schmitt looks out at us from time, asserting the elemental kinship, the Biglens live in their own time, and the painting is a perception of transcendent possibility there. [*See note, page 284.*]

In *The Biglen Brothers Racing (Figure 13),* done in 1873, though time may not be the central theme, there is an effect which we associate with it. The race itself appears to be the focus of attention, and yet the drama of racing is muted. The effect may be of the dark water, of the light on the blade of an oar, of the brothers' isolation — there are spectators barely seen on the shore and on the excursion boat, and there is the bow of another scull in the foreground, but they are alone with their skill — through which Eakins communicates his feeling that in the presence of activity, sustained by water, seen in a full summer light that seems to stand for the high tide of physical maturity for these men, one comes to face the sadness of the purely natural world, redeemed only by quiet human action, by devotion to some task. The fragile shell stretches the length of the canvas. The moment is frozen again, and the full presence, the coming on of humanity, implies here the possibility, the certainty of absence too. So that Eakins' sense of time is once more the distinguishing element of his view of the natural world, a view which begins simply in a loving response to physical sport on the river.

The largest of these paintings, *The Biglen Brothers Turning the Stake* (1873) *(Figure 14)* is, in its mood and color, less evocative of the sense of melancholy than the others. The two sweating, muscular men are more nearly the subjects of the painting; John Biglen, upright at the number one oar, Barney looking down, an intensity in his posture and his concentration. In the stake boat, in the left middle distance, Eakins, his right hand raised, holds the starter's pistol.

It is as if he were observing epic heroes at their games. The riverscape and the distant bank crowded with spectators form an arena in which the brothers are both isolated and magnified. A moment in history has been made timeless. There is no irony in Eakins' view of the professional sportsmen of his time; he sees only a nobility in their effort, their control, their dedication. They responded to victory one feels, in the style of Greeks accepting prizes after

13. THE BIGLEN BROTHERS RACING
1873. 24 x 36. National Gallery of Art, Washington, D.C. Gift of Mr. and Mrs. Cornelius Vanderbilt Whitney.

14. THE BIGLEN BROTHERS TURNING THE STAKE
1873. 40 x 60. The Cleveland Museum of Art, Hinman B. Hurlbut Collection.

their epic games. . . . To the right, passing out of the picture, and preceding them into history, is a paddle-wheeled steamer. [*See note, page 285.*]

WITH an instinct, and by the largeness of his conscious intention, Eakins was forming that very personal style which avoided the inflated and the grandiose as it did a loss in realistic minutiae and the possibilities of the trivial. The romantic elements of his temperament were bound up with a perception that might more suggestively be described as classic than as realistic — the images of mutability inextricable from images of stability, strength, order. Together, in the rowing scenes, these elements of his nature produced the effect of suspended time — as if the painter himself were looking back upon images of a past era — which Gérôme could not understand when he criticized the "immobility" of a rower in the middle of a stroke, and which strikes occasional critics today who are disturbed by the "static" quality of Eakins' work. What caught Eakins' eye were the faces and postures of men seen in landscapes simultaneously fixed and changing. He saw character in time, and the rest followed.

An inheritor of the Jacksonian tradition in celebrating the common man, Eakins is even more significantly part of the Emersonian in the depth of his response to the significant reality of the close at hand. The dramatic possibilities of his first paintings were realized when he conveyed his sense of the tension between men or women and their environment, whether of Victorian America of the Brown Decades or of a timeless late nineteenth-century America rapidly becoming history. Embracing the common in his genre work, Eakins, like Emerson, was asserting connections with larger realities.

Genre painting ordinarily does not carry philosophic weight, though nothing has ever prevented it from doing so. Typically, its men and women are not seen as individuals, but as examples. In Philadelphia, genre work, like portraiture, was acceptable if it made neither intellectual nor moral demands of the picture viewer, if it implied no serious view of existence, if it was pleasant, picturesque, and anecdotal in a simple-minded way. Eakins' work made its demands. It was built upon intellectual and psychological awarenesses, especially in the idea of a relation between subject and environment, uncommon in American painting of that time. If it was pictorially pleasing, it had to be regarded seriously; it demanded an attention to its meanings as well as to its more apparent moods.

American genre painting might express optimism, sentimentality, humor, nostalgia, but above all it expressed innocence, even in the fine work of Mount, of Bingham, of Blythe. Painting his men and women in democratic postures, in these posed probings of unconscious gesture against the ordinary backgrounds of this quiet civilization, Eakins discovers his deeply felt and, one is tempted to say, prophetic response to reality through his observation of recognizable individuals. Yet neither landscape nor interior is mere stage for human statement; in the tension between man and his natural or created environment, and in the subtle expressions of that tension there is an undertone of affirmation that is more than merely emotional, implying the significance of personal human existence, a respect for the manifestations of consciousness revealed in a particular time and place. In the early work especially one feels that this undertone flows from Eakins' loving response to landscape and interior as well as to the men and women he pictures. These paintings have the spiritual quality which one associates with Northern art; the tension between consciousness and environment, the almost tangibly evoked atmosphere, is always made to imply something larger about human existence.

The Artist and His Father Hunting Reed Birds (Figure 15), painted in 1874, shows a gently ironic, almost comic falling away from this tension. The serious questing figures have a mock epic quality as they move in a landscape which threatens them in no way. The artist is awkwardly off-balance as he poles his father toward some defenseless quarry. Benjamin Eakins in his high-crowned heavy-brimmed hat is all competence, yet there is a sweet naïveté in him as he watches for opportunity. At the left, behind father and son, are an upright pusher and a hunter, his head down as he cleans his gun. There is a double movement in some of this work as Eakins reduces his heroes to scale, and simultaneously asserts their human significance.

Pushing for Rail of the same year *(Figure 16)* has six important paired figures and a dozen less significant ones in the background. The massive pusher and the hunter at the right are balanced by the potbellied man on the left. The central figures of the dark hunter ejecting a shell and of the Negro pusher looking out are the slightest, physically, and the most impressive. With his quiet wit Eakins moves a step beyond what he has classically attained here — a feeling for the muted greens and golds of landscape set against a gray-blue sky (the easy winds are felt only by their effect upon distant sails) — to take the American sportsman's humanity seriously, yet

15. THE ARTIST AND HIS FATHER HUNTING REED BIRDS
ON THE COHANSEY MARSHES
1874. 18 x 27. Collection of Mr. and Mrs. Paul Mellon.

16. PUSHING FOR RAIL
1874. 13 x 30. The Metropolitan Museum of Art, Arthur H. Hearn Fund, 1916.

17. WHISTLING FOR PLOVER
1874. Watercolor. 16½ x 11. The Brooklyn Museum.

18. STARTING OUT AFTER RAIL

1874. 24 x 20. Museum of Fine Arts, Boston (Hayden Collection).

19. SAILBOATS (HIKERS) RACING ON THE DELAWARE
1874. 24 x 36. Collection of the Philadelphia Museum of Art.

20. BECALMED ON THE DELAWARE

1874. 10⅛ x 17¼. Collection of the Philadelphia Museum of Art.

again quietly to mock — and it is almost too strong a word — his adventure. In lesser hands either scene would have slipped over into the competence of illustration or the banalities of anecdote.

There were other paintings at this time in the same genre, including the 1874 *Whistling for Plover (Figure 17)*. In *Starting Out After Rail* of the same year *(Figure 18)* the intent is more serious. The critic who described one version of the painting (at the Boston Museum of Fine Arts) was impressed by what he called its naturalism, its faithfulness to detail. He found pleasure in remarking "the light touch of the hand of the man at the tiller, the stretch of his trousers across the seat, the shine of his companion's boots in the sun, the double-barrelled shotgun in the bottom of the boat, the reflection and the shadows of the sails in the shoal water, the large boats making their way in the Delaware's channel, the blue haze of land through the gap." The effect of the whole was open to question, however. "The emptiness of the sky is perhaps disappointing, and that is where Eakins' weakness lies. His absorption with details often became so great that he frequently failed to organize them into a unified whole."

Despite the critic, the emptiness of sky has its meaning and its effect. Here, as in the sculling scenes, men are isolated physically and frozen in motion. The relative calm of the Delaware and the unseen wind can be felt in their opposition. As the boat swings away, one of the men turns to look back at the viewer and the painting is centered in that glance as it was in Max Schmitt's direct scrutiny. The effect of human connections so unexpectedly asserted is given force by the almost oppressive emptiness of sky. Eakins began his preparation for the painting by defining space and the position of the boat through a perspective drawing. The men in the boat were his friends Harry Young and Sam Helhower. But the painting's effect transcends any concern for fact as it does its successes in technique and in portraiture.

In *Sailboats (Hikers) Racing on the Delaware (Figure 19)* and in *Becalmed on the Delaware (Figure 20)*, both painted in 1874, men become less significant than nature observed in a quiet mood. In the first, he is concerned with the movement of air and water felt and measured by men, and in the second, with the absence of movement in a waterscape where the reduced figures of men are the measures of space and nothing more. The central figure of *Hikers* tends his sheets and looks up at the luff of the mainsail — at the force of the breeze felt by it. His bulk, his gesture, and his old clothes individualize him; he is a receiver of life, not a maker, controlling the wind's momentary and small effect, neither dominating the moment nor communicating out of it, totally absorbed in contemplation of the wind. The muddy darkness of Delaware water and the grayish-blue color of a windy day complete the painting's mood.

The small *Becalmed on the Delaware* marks, it would seem, an interval of peace in Eakins' life and an affirmation. The sailing ships are at some distance, almost more felt than seen; once more time is simultaneously suspended and receding in this moment, and once more Eakins appears conscious of recording something of an era fast becoming history. His friends disappear from the waterscapes and air and light become his subjects exclusively.

The world he pictures in and about Philadelphia is never a harsh one, and I feel it especially true of Eakins that the representation of light in all his work is an expression of love. Painters in a more orthodox religious tradition could give their unqualified assent to the sentiment of Sebastian Frank, the sixteenth-century mystic whom Sir Kenneth Clark quotes in *Landscape into Art:* "As the air fills everything and is not confined to one place, as the light of the sun overfloods the whole earth, so God dwells in everything and everything dwells in Him." There is in the vivid sense of air and light in these paintings some substitute, by way of the painter's purely human love for his subjects, for the God who is absent from them. Nor does Eakins accept a faith in nature for a faith in God. Air and sun form the impalpable substance of light in which men and women can be felt solidly and fully for their brief moments. "Facts become art through love, which unifies them and lifts them to a higher plane of reality; and in landscapes this all embracing love is expressed by light." For Eakins, if light is love it is also time, and the classic sobriety of these paintings even in their more light-hearted moments is hardly to be felt apart from an essential sadness.

4

ALTERNATE qualities of Eakins' temperament affirmed themselves in the portraits and in the sculling scenes painted before *The Gross Clinic.* The strong intuitive element of his nature drew him to Rembrandt and to Velásquez in his portraiture, and then, alternately, to Gérôme when he wished to express the seemingly objective sense of bodies and objects in space characteristic of his paintings of men rowing on the Schuylkill. Did technique and intuition achieve closer correspondence in the one than in the other? In the sculling scenes the preparatory methods and even something of the technique of Gérôme produced their memorable effect — that of men and objects caught in space and time, fixed yet passing, and a sense of disparity, perhaps, only when one feels that the epic and heroic qualities of a painting might have achieved fuller expression in a bolder canvas.

But it must appear, the whole of Eakins' work considered, that the more open method was more fundamental to his nature, more suitable to the expression of a force feminine in the depth of its intuitions, masculine in the expression of its power. The open method did away with the preparatory drawing and made use of the oil sketch grounded more directly in intuition than in reason and calculation. "You guess at it," Eakins would later tell his students, "and then correct it and try to get it right." He worked and taught his students to work directly with the brush. [*See note, page 285.*]

When Eakins sent Gérôme an example of his work, it was a watercolor of a rower, not a portrait. But a watercolor could no more suggest the full possibilities of his art than the methods of Gérôme might have served as the basis for his power over a lifetime. The small figure of the rower achieved something of the response he had hoped for, and Gérôme wrote him, "*Je suis bien enchanté que mes conseils, appliqués quoique tardivement, aient enfin portés leurs fruits.*" The earlier "*inquiétude*" of the master had been largely stilled though he objected to Eakins' showing his rower in the middle of a stroke. Eakins corrected that "error" with another watercolor and his master found it entirely good, though now he wondered whether work of that sort was "*commerciale.*" It was not.

When he sought to directly engage the public interest for the first time, he threw over the method of Gérôme for the bolder more vital approach, trusting himself to the kind of intuition Bergson was later to define, that formative quality of the unconscious which may break through, with luck, after some kind of intellectual preparation. The most dramatic example of this intuition at work, the sketch, made in 1875, for *The Gross Clinic (Figure 21)* is, in effect, a work of memory based upon untold hours of observation. In later years Eakins himself looked upon this sketch with a kind of wonder. From the dark world of that small canvas flashes of light break out, the gray-haired figure in the center, the figures of men seemingly crouched beneath him, and one has the sense of form and life discovering themselves, a kind of Genesis.

As a young doctor, Samuel Gross had gone to New York City at the height of a plague, to observe its course, and to make his report on the dead and the dying.

At the age of twenty-eight, in 1833, he went to Cincinnati as demonstrator in anatomy at the Medical College of Ohio, where his two letters of introduction to well-known doctors were ignored. After this, he wrote, "I never accepted a letter of introduction to anyone, having independence enough to rely upon my own resources and address for advancement in my profession. I, however, soon carved my way."

He was sensitive of his public reputation and felt it necessary to make its foundation quite plain. "Persons have often come to me saying that they had understood that I was fond of using the knife. . . . Nothing could be more untrue or more unjust. No man ever had a greater or more unmitigated contempt for the knife's man, or mere mechanical surgeon and operator, than I, and I have never hesitated, in season and out of season, to denounce him. I have performed many operations, and flatter myself that I possess at least some of the qualities of a good operator — a steady hand, an unflinching eye, perfect self-control, and a thorough knowledge of relative anatomy." Eakins could appreciate those qualities, as important to the painter as they were to the surgeon.

21. SKETCH FOR THE GROSS CLINIC
1875. 24 x 20. Collection of the Philadelphia Museum of Art.

22. THE GROSS CLINIC
1875. 96 x 78. Jefferson Medical College, Philadelphia.

Samuel Gross was of the breed of remarkable, lucky men who find release through great expenditures of energy in unabating devotion to work whose significance cannot be questioned. There was place neither for soul's doubt nor for fatigue of body in this man's universe. We are inclined, in Eakins' later portraits, to read the era into the faces of the men he paints. How much of the era expresses itself through the head of Samuel Gross?

Six years before Eakins painted him, the famous doctor and teacher examined himself. "Am I old at sixty-four? I do not feel that I am. If my vigor has in any degree abated, I am not conscious of it. I have just finished my thirtieth course of lectures on surgery. If I ever lectured better, with greater enthusiasm, or with more point and effect, with more ease and unction than I have this winter, I am not aware of it."

He was seventy years old when Eakins painted him in his clinic, and two years later was still able to congratulate himself upon his continuing good health. His sight was excellent, and his hand as steady as ever. His reflections upon death befitted the man of hard good sense. "When I am dead I should like to be burned. . . . I have a great respect for urn burial, and hope the day is not distant when it will come into general use. I know no more disagreeable sight than a graveyard, especially in a city."

Eakins was the inheritor of the same strain of iron and uncorrupted self-reliance. He had the same force and many of the same qualities of character, and had he become a physician, as he once thought he might, those qualities should have found similar release. But the age which favored the development of individualism in science, in business, and in industry, had no use for it in art, and Eakins at seventy presents a more battered appearance than does Samuel Gross.

In 1875 Eakins, a young man fully conscious of his own ability, chose to make the surgeon the subject of his most ambitious work, one that would exhibit the full power he had largely restrained thus far. He was certain that the painting of Dr. Gross in his clinic would establish his reputation and so open the way to the development of his art. The painting of a similar subject had done that for the young Rembrandt, and Eakins possibly had the example in mind.

In *The Gross Clinic (Figure 22)* the famous surgeon in his black frock coat stands at the apex of a pyramid of light in which a team of surgeons are assisting in an operation, successive pyramids of forms building to that brilliantly executed head. Virgil Barker speaks of the sense of ritualistic drama conveyed by "the bold and grail-like light in the midst of the mystery of shadow." In that light, the powerful assertion of an uncompromising humanism achieves something paradoxically like religious intensity. There is something in the painting's undertone reminiscent of a Descent from the Cross, with God himself present.

The Gross Clinic is so important in the history of American art because it raises realistic American subject matter to the level of myth with a broad and profound power and an intelligence that had never been approached before. The depth of Eakins' penetration of his subject can most be felt in the head of the surgeon. His intellect did not permit him to paint a high priest of the religion of science, the embodiment of a romantic and unqualified affirmation of the will. For the great surgeon is in part the victim of his own power. In the drama being enacted in the amphitheater Dr. Gross, poised in this moment with life flowing beneath him, caught up between contemplation and action, mediating like some god between the detachment of his students and the techniques of his assistants, dominates this community by personal force and through the intensity of his vision. And at the height of this intellectual passion he is almost lost to feeling.

When he was commissioned to paint the portraits of Nicolaas Tulp and of the directors of the Amsterdam Guild of Surgeons in 1631, Rembrandt was working in established social and aesthetic traditions. [*See note, page 285.*] Eakins' creative and social problems were more complex. Sustained by no tradition, creating, in effect, vision where none had been, his breakthrough is the more dramatic and the more impressive.

For the Philadelphian of the time, the heroic painting might celebrate great men or great events, preferably military or political. Dr. Gross may have carved his way to eminence, but Philadelphia could not be troubled by exhibitions of his personal force carried on in a charity clinic. To picture any surgeon spattered with blood, the bloody scalpel in his bloody hand, was an offense to an audience which wished to be ennobled by other sorts of images. Blood could be expected in a battle scene but not in a work that spoke so strongly of the pains of mortality. Eakins' audience wished to be reminded neither of human suffering nor of the agonies of the flesh.

Something else disturbed genteel Philadelphia. In the better known of Rembrandt's anatomy lessons, *The Anatomy of Dr. Tulp*, the corpse is stretched out from right to left on the canvas, its loins covered with a cloth, and although it is seen from below and foreshortened, it causes no difficulty to the spectator. By contrast, the position of the patient in *The Gross Clinic*, seen in effect from a seat in the amphitheater at virtually the same level as the operating table, is not at all easy to understand. The soles of the patient's feet, covered with a towel, are turned toward us and his knees are flexed to present his bare thigh to the picture viewer. Limbs, trunk and head, radically foreshortened and masked by operating cloths, the view of the patient broken up by the hands and arms of the assistants — these were elements of a human and an aesthetic mystery. If a good Philadelphian could look long enough to solve that mystery, his scrutiny brought him no comfort. The unaccustomed pose was offensive; he found himself contemplating the patient's left buttock and his anus.

Horror and indignation were voiced by Philadelphia's newspapers which came loudly to the defense of injured sensibilities and of "high art." When Eakins exhibited the work in downtown Philadelphia, the painting was called "brutal," "a degradation of art," an offense to "the innate delicacy of our people." The rhetorical image of "the people" was as unreal as the genteel response was unseeing. "As to people with weak stomachs and strong nerves the scene is so real that they might as well go to a dissecting room and have done with it." Eakins' work was, at best, "a picture which strong men find it difficult to look at long." Eakins had anticipated this sort of response, in a sense, with the figure of the patient's mother who covers her face, unable to look at the scene. [*See note, page 285.*]

R. P. Blackmur has pointed out in some connection that talent seldom expresses the right thing at the right time in the right place. He was wrong. Talent is always correct. Genius is required to stand this far ahead of its time and to make this sort of trouble for itself.

Although a solitary critic of the time was convinced that "nothing in the line of portraiture that has ever been attempted in this city or indeed in this country . . . in any way approaches it," his judgment carried no weight. Eakins was long dead before the work achieved any popular recognition in Philadelphia. Some seventy-five years after he painted it, during a celebration of the Philadelphia Museum's seventy-fifth anniversary, *The Gross Clinic* received the third highest number of votes in a popularity contest. It ranked, interestingly, behind Rubens, represented by *The Flight of Lot and his Family*, and behind El Greco's *View of Toledo*.

By that time the audience had assimilated what it took to be the painting's theme and had, indeed, seen the idea become a commonplace—the communal fight against death and disease led by one of the new heroes of science. Or they could read it as a painting with historical interest, showing doctors at work in their dark suits before the development of antisepsis. James Flexner thought Dr. Gross "one of the most heroic figures in American art," and Robert Henri told his students to look at the painting for the "stupendous romance of real life," and none of these impressions was incorrect. Yet taken alone or taken collectively they still do not point to the center of the painting's force, and they might as easily apply to Sir Luke Fildes' *The Doctor*, an even more popular work which never offended anyone, as far as I know.

For tragic implications in a dramatic work, for the revolutionary quality of his vision, Eakins was never to surpass *The Gross Clinic*, and it was not that he was personally unequal to moving beyond it. One thinks of Melville making use of what Matthiessen calls "the living facts of ordinary existence . . . [as] the source of whatever heroic myths Americans can live by" only to be called a madman for the greatest work of his imagination. In truth, the living facts of *ordinary* existence are no more to be found in Dr. Gross's operating amphitheater than they are aboard the *Pequod*, no more than the myths discovered there were to be accessible to ordinary men. If Melville's imagination and Eakins' (though this is hardly the usual view of him) worked with the conviction that certain of the data of existence were the materials of larger meaning, these meanings were to be unseen, misconstrued or found offensive by genteel America. At thirty-one, Melville and Eakins had been, each in his turn, mistaken in the judgment of his audience, for each of these masterpieces implies the existence of men capable of some degree of understanding and appreciation. But the "old genteel America," in Santayana's terms, "eager to know the truth and to be 'cultured' and to love 'art' and to miss nothing that made other nations interesting or distinguished" was handicapped by "the meagreness of soul and its thinness of temper and its paucity of talent, [and] it *could* not attain nor even approach any of those ideals." One associates the kind of introspection and deeply serious intention of which Melville and Eakins were capable with the best part of their Protestant inheritance, and the kinds of response to their works with the customary darknesses of that same tradition. The reception of *The Gross Clinic*, no less than that of *Moby Dick*, is a classic illustration of the shipwreck of the imagination in nineteenth-century America. Eakins survived as an artist, though his art was undoubtedly turned from the broader course it might have taken had there been an audience equal to it.

Of all American cities, Philadelphia is the least given to radicalism, and sure always to be found safe, prudent, moderate, and what is known in England as liberal conservative.

—*North American*, February 14, 1876

In what is termed high art, it cannot be said that American soil discloses the footprints of a coming man.

— Edward C. Bruce, *The Century, Its Fruits and Its Festival*, Philadelphia, 1877

IN 1876 Philadelphia was sprawled over some one hundred and twenty-nine square miles, the largest city in the world in extent. Twenty-three and one-half miles long, eight miles wide at its widest, it was bounded on the northeast by Bucks County; on the east and southeast by the Delaware River; on the south by Delaware County; on the north and northwest by Montgomery County. In 1870 it was the second city of the United States in population; by 1876 that population had risen to 817,000. The city had spilled beyond the limits of the two rivers that had originally formed its natural boundaries.

A typical house was of pressed brick with wide marble steps and facings, and with solid wooden shutters painted white. Pavements were of brick; streets were largely unpaved, or paved with Belgian blocks.

First among the cities in number of manufacturing establishments, in capital investment, in hands employed, in wages paid, in materials used, only New York exceeded it in the value of its products. It was celebrated for its banks and railroads, the two forms of corporate enterprise which were felt to have achieved perfection.

By 1876 moral perfection had been achieved by the newspapers which exercised it in defense of purity in the arts. Alex McClure, publisher of the *Times*, an advocate of high moral tone in the arts, found the theaters of his time "indecent, obscene, and disgusting." The arrival of Offenbach in Philadelphia produced a crisis. A reviewer in the *Bulletin* attacked his operetta *La Jolie Parfumeuse*, and called Offenbach "a glorifier of filth." Never in the critic's memory had he "descended to greater depths of obscenity." The *Press* found *Measure for Measure* by an earlier and even more immodest writer "utterly unfit for presentation."

Moral perfection had not been achieved elsewhere than in the newspapers. In politics morality had no role. The Eakinses were Democrats at this time though the city was largely Republican. It was in general difficult to vote against the party that had preserved the Union. It made no difference if one did. A Republican ring, casting the votes of children, dogs, and the signers of the Declaration of Independence, controlled the city's power in politics through the tax office, the gas trust, the highway department and the police.

THE Congress of the United States by an act approved March 3, 1871, provided that the centennial anniversary of the Declaration of American Independence in Philadelphia should be celebrated in that city "by holding an International Exhibition of Arts, Manufactures, and products of the soil and mine."

It was the Gilded Age and the age of Grant, and if it was still largely an agrarian world, its centers of interest and of force were shifting rapidly. Interestingly, though the Philadelphia Exhibition emphasized machinery and the future of industrial America, the bulk of its visitors were drawn to Memorial Hall where they pondered the grandiose landscape and the picturesque views of an earlier age. Built at the cost of one and a half million dollars, Memorial Hall had an art annex of thirty galleries, each forty feet square, and one larger room. The length of wall covered with pictures was estimated to be two and a half miles. Industrial America was not pictured there.

The guide to the gallery sought to define the prospects for art in this country. "The American people exhibit to a large degree a high appreciation of works of art, and the United States is found one of the best picture markets in the world. With the increase of wealth, a corresponding desire for the possession of paintings and statuary is found to exist. The cultivation of the aesthetic instincts of the masses is becoming daily more apparent, and the Centennial Exhibition will do more to elevate in a brief period the tastes of our citizens than could be possibly accomplished during many years of ordinary exertion."

Meanwhile those who could afford true art collected chinoiserie, japonica, and the modern French school. The banker James L. Claghorn, "had spent a fortune on the finest line engravings, mezzotints and etchings to be found in Europe." He sold his oils to buy more engravings.

Philadelphia was the proper place for a great exhibition of art. It was thought of as the cradle of art in America, as an art center, and there were those who praised it for the strong aesthetic tone pervading social life. The Philadelphia *Press* explained its taste in painting: "Philadelphians like to see the work of Philadelphians especially when the artist was of the old quiet modest families that have done so much to build up our good city and maintain its highest standard for integrity and persistent but unobtrusive work." The function of True Art was to delight and instruct, of course, and if it tried to do that, one might attempt to overlook any aesthetic deficiencies — that was the counsel of the *Weekly Guide to the Exhibition*. "True American specimens of Art, no matter how much there might be to deplore about them, would at least be in keeping with our appreciation and advancement, and this should satisfy all reasonable needs."

Edward Bruce, chronicler of the festival, surveyed the scene and reported, with some satisfaction, that "Stuart, Sully, Neagle and Inman stand on as yet unshaken pedestals." He was at the same time sure that "the social position of the artist never was higher," though he did not inquire into what that could mean.

Scattered among the paintings on the walls of Memorial Hall were five by Thomas Eakins. *The Chess Players (Figure 27)* was among the pictures commended for merit in genre painting. The others went unnoticed — the portrait of Rand *(Figure 10)*, and the watercolor *Baseball* and *Whistling for Plover (Figure 17)*. No. 249 in the Exhibition, in the Great Cow tradition, was the *Return of the Herd* by Peter Moran, Philadelphia, distinguished as a "powerful picture" by the catalog. It replaced *The Gross Clinic (Figure 22)*, a more disturbing work, which was hung in the medical section by the guardians of tone (moral, aesthetic, and nervous) among the exhibits of trusses, artificial limbs, and ear cleaners.

I can conceive of few circumstances wherein I would have to paint a woman naked.

—Eakins in a letter to his father, 1867

GIVEN the beginnings of his career as we have seen them, the decade between 1876 and 1886 was in many ways the most crucial to Eakins and the most central to the meaning of his life and of his art. The mood underlying his genre work and his landscapes generally remains one of affection and of love for the world he pictures. In his portraits of the mid-to-late seventies, of Harry Lewis and of Dr. Brinton *(Figures 23 and 24)*, for instance, the psychological realism which was to emerge after a decade or more as the major element of his work began to reveal the lines it might take. But what continued to distinguish much of the other work was its deeply felt though always restrained feeling, its lyricism, even its romanticism, as Eakins absorbed the moods of his subjects. Beyond this, his painting continued to show its highly sophisticated concern for beauty. Facts were subordinated to a larger vision; beauty and vision were inseparable. Atmosphere and mood ordered the facts; objects had meanings within larger intellectual and emotional schemes.

He painted the life he knew, but one can always measure the separation between what he knew and what he chose to print. The facts of his life were not the subjects of most of his paintings. For Eakins the crucial public events of this time were the beginning of his teaching, in 1876, his rise to a position of social force as Director of Instruction at the Pennsylvania Academy of Fine Arts in 1882, and his dismissal from that position in 1886, after a decade of teaching essentially in conflict with the mores and desires of the social order which controlled the Academy. The crucial private events of his life

23. HARRY LEWIS
1876. 24 x 20. Collection of the Philadelphia Museum of Art.

24. DR. JOHN H. BRINTON
1876. 78⅜ x 57⅛. National Gallery of Art, Washington, D.C., on loan from the Armed Forces Institute of Pathology.

were the deaths of his fiancée, Katherine Crowell, in 1879, of his sister Margaret, in 1882, and his marriage to Susan Hannah Macdowell in 1884.

Toward the end of the decade he celebrated his marriage with another of the great and crucial portraits of American painting, one which probed a world and a consciousness as no American portrait had done before. The preparation for it had gone on largely underground. But between 1876 and 1885 his work had been only intermittently inspired by the kind of insight that had erupted in *The Gross Clinic (Figure 22)*. It is as if he had by a violent effort of repression turned away from too intense a scrutiny of the forces shaping life, or as if he were not yet prepared to do so. He had no taste for the landscapes of his city or for the outward forms of a civilization fast industrializing. In that decade he continued to paint the landscapes of a passing agrarian civilization, the last of an era when fishermen still worked at their nets in the Delaware.

He also painted a dozen or more genre studies which, while they display his affection for past or passing elements of a quiet agrarian world and are small masterpieces of mood and atmosphere, are not central to his vision, not expressive of the great force which was to discover release in more powerful ways. Consider the subjects of some of these paintings and sketches: *In Grandmother's Time; Young Girl Meditating; The Courtship; Retrospection (Figure 25); A Quiet Moment; Spinning (Figure 26)*. They were innocuous works and they found favor with the genteel. President Seelye bought one for the newly founded Smith College, and two others won prizes. We associate their themes with Eakins, and he handles them with his accustomed gravity, and even with a gentle lyricism, yet they lack the qualities of intensity which distinguish his greatest work. They were works at the periphery of his consciousness or, in harsher terms, works of emasculation. He posed Margaret in the *spinning* scenes which have their charm surely, but where is the promise in these small atmospheric works of the family portraits painted after his return from Europe and the Prado? Force was lost in the quest for delicacy. Margaret's death in 1882 shook him profoundly. She might well have been the subject of some very great paintings. Instead he had painted small watercolors of her graceful figure, with her head turned away from the spectator or looking down modestly at her work.

The painting of this entire decade, in its avoidance of the themes which were at the center of his consciousness, provides evidence of the powerful personal and public repressions under which he labored. In the decade between the completion of *The Gross Clinic* and his resignation from the Academy, he produced no more significant work than he had in half that time after his return from Europe. Restraint as an element of his art too easily became repression of force. Again, the teacher very nearly swamped the artist, for the slowdown of creativity and the repression of force had as much to do with his teaching as with the regrettable "lesson" of *The Gross Clinic*. He was a great teacher, and suffered from the corollary of that condition. His thinking was essentially subversive of the moral order of his time; yet he essayed a social role as the director of an institution in which he was bound to find himself hung up between the demands of his art and the small-minded decorum of that world. His insistence upon the nude in his teaching was a call to honesty in a world which relished appearance and the outward forms of behavior.

In a life so outwardly uneventful, in a career so apparently dominated by high intention, the uncertain elements of existence — the tentative, the crucial, the moments of crisis — compete in our mind's eye with what we may take as the inexorable history of genius seeing its way, choosing its path, discovering its ultimate vocation. And in the competition life becomes fluid once more, or more precisely, we become conscious of its tensions once more, of the sober consciousness regarding its world, making its choices, and of the world forcing life along unsought ways. The form of freedom is shaped by imposed necessity, the seer's destiny formed by his world. Eakins had his freedom thrust upon him. No man was more bound and more free than he.

When in 1876 in *The Chess Players (Figure 27)* he tried another tack in the quest for public approbation, he chose methods unlike those employed in *The Gross Clinic (Figure 22)*. He painted a small work meant to demonstrate his mastery of genre, a painting calculated to offend no one.

Is *The Chess Players* a disappointment only because it is so great a retreat from the promise of *The Gross Clinic?* The power, the expansiveness, the priestly quality of that painting give way to the controlled observation of three higher representatives of a middle-class world, all formally dressed. Again Eakins forms a pyramid of human figures; now its apex is the head of Benjamin Eakins, not dominating the scene, but participating in the mood of quiet scholarly concentration. Yet even here power and vision have not given way to mere sentimental feeling for the amenities and decencies of this world, for the painting masters mood and atmosphere with a certainty and a delicacy rare enough in American painting.

25. RETROSPECTION
1880. 14½ x 10⅛. Yale University Art Gallery, bequest of Stephen C. Clark.

26. SPINNING
1881. Watercolor. 11 x 8. Mrs. John R. Garrett, Sr.

27. THE CHESS PLAYERS
1876. 11¾ x 16¾. The Metropolitan Museum of Art, Gift of the Artist, 1881.

The teacher of French, the painter and the writing master are older men, the two seated men almost fragile in the late-afternoon sunlight. The themes of fragility and time underlie the more obvious ones. On the small table are half-filled decanters and glasses; on the mantel, an ornate clock. Solidity and order are set against time, and the small circle of this room against the world outside, marked by the water pipe, the landscape above the mantel, and the globe. Through this concentrated yet undemonstrative mastery of subject, of atmosphere, and of mood, Eakins communicates his sense of deep affection for this world. The size of the painting is a reminder that love was being purchased at some cost.

Although the psychological motive of *The Chess Players* — the reading of character in that quiet environment — is not unimportant, the painting could not provide the scope for any searching insight into consciousness. One of the most effective of the early portraits, in this respect, is that of Dr. John H. Brinton *(Figure 24)*, painted in 1876, in which Eakins used the full-length life-size canvas to pursue human meaning directly and forcefully. The painting again measures an area of civilization as well as a man. It is the dusky, stable world of *The Chess Players* with its heavy dark furniture and its oriental rugs, and Dr. Brinton, successor to the chair of Dr. Gross, was one of its best representatives, a strong, impressive figure, a Philadelphian of uncommon ability and vitality. It is not an unalloyed strength that we see here for there is a fatigue in that appearance, and in this moment of fading light Dr. Brinton, facing the spectator so directly, also appears to confront some deeper meaning in his own existence. The portrait discovers contrary possibilities of existence in a way that *The Chess Players* could not, and its affirmations are the more powerful. Light falls upon the man's lined face, upon his strong relaxed hands, his writing materials on the desk to his right, and upon the open book on the reading stand to his left. A younger man's portrait hangs in the upper right; Dr. Brinton's name is on a discarded envelope in an urnlike basket in the lower left.

The portrait measures strength of character, dominating this room as it had dominated Dr. Brinton's own experience, against a weariness of the flesh and the erosions of time, the self-assurance of the professional man against an understanding of the sadness of existence, the naturalistic impression against an assertion of the value of moral force. As a witness to the victory of character Eakins engages in no show of optimism. There is no rhetorical inflation in the painting; its sober restraint is inseparable from its power.

Interestingly, the mood of sober psychological inquiry — simultaneously grounded in a searching naturalism and in larger convictions about the importance of character — did not dominate this period. And again, though the intellectual quality of Eakins' work is always important, it may be less overtly expressed at this time than some kind of direct response to the world, in which meanings are seemingly discovered after the impressions and after the fact. The feeling and the meanings of *The Chess Players* were for the time more characteristic than the deep human questioning of the *Brinton.* What is so impressive in either case, whether a work appears to have been dominated by some direct intellectual or emotional impression, are the possibilities of treatment, the diversity of meanings and effects he can achieve in a range of subjects that is not so narrow after all.

When he moved out of doors for these subjects he was even less concerned than he had been two or three years before to record literal impressions of landscape, and one feels ever more certainly that it was his response to beauty and his simultaneous apprehension of theme that ordered his work and not the facts themselves. The life-size full-length portrait of his two-year-old niece Ella Crowell, the *Baby at Play* (1876) *(Figure 28)* in the sunlight outside the house on Mt. Vernon Street, is full of a sense of sober joy, and the enveloping mood of love gives life to the precise forms of things recorded there. The child is soberly at play, abstracted as she reaches for a block on the red-brick walk. Gesture and posture are intuitions beyond fact, as are the forms of the flowerpot, the doll, the alphabet blocks, and the toy horse and cart moving away. The sunlight bathing everything in warmth, revealing the fullness of the child's body and playing upon the rich green of the background becomes a metaphor for love and for wonder. The richness of the moment is fully realized in that suspended morning light. Yet there is no sentimentality in the effect; this delightful painting rather draws one into its meditative mood, achieving its effects through that tension of emotional response and restraint that was so strong a quality of Eakins' temperament.

It is typical of his work that the meditative mood can be discovered in places where one might not expect it in a lesser artist, in this portrait of a baby at play, or in a hunting scene such as the 1876 *Will Schuster and Blackman Going Shooting (Figure 29).* In restoring the human figure to a central place in the landscape (after those works in the early seventies in which it had all but disappeared) Eakins chose to confront a new meaning, the identity and individuality of a Negro who would have been a stereotyped figure in the work of most other artists of the period. There is a dignity and a

28. BABY AT PLAY

1876. 32¼ x 48. From the Collection of Mr. and Mrs. John Hay Whitney.

29. WILL SCHUSTER AND BLACKMAN GOING SHOOTING
1876. 22⅛ x 30¼. Yale University Art Gallery, bequest of Stephen C. Clark.

strength in the figure of the Negro pushing the skiff eastward through the green marshland, standing there in his bare feet, his knees flexed as he works the pole. It is the portrait of an intelligence at one with its environment. Eakins paints hands, Will Schuster's holding the gun, Blackman's probing with the pole, with a certainty that here stands for the mastery of environment by these men.

The subdued light of early morning in *Will Schuster and Blackman* gives way in *The Fairman Rogers Four-in-Hand (Figure 30)* of 1879, to a stronger light used to illuminate the solid forms of figures in a landscape and to create a mood of an entirely different sort, one whose force derives from the subjective response to a realistic subject matter. There is sunlight on the road, on the faces of the coaching party and on the rich greens of grass and trees. The vitality of the painting lies in an objective scrutiny now in tension with an intuition of the atmosphere of time that is quite different from anything in *Baby at Play* or *Will Schuster and Blackman Going Shooting*. Air and sunlight may suggest release, but the habit of restraint again shows itself in this intense study of light and suspended movement. The painting's monumental forms are set against symbols of time and change — the massed figures on the coach, the masonry of the culvert, and the coach against the road in sunlight, the movement of the coach, the sunlight itself. Time and mortality are not placed in opposition as they were in the rowing scenes; the vision of an entire class now becomes focal — and so he paints the almost harshly realistic miniature portraits of family and servants. (Apart from the portraits of Rogers and of his brother-in-law, there is nothing very engaging in the faces or attitudes of the others on the coach.) It is the vision of an order, of energy harnessed for social display, of forces stable, yet passing into time and history. [*See note, page 285.*]

Fairman Rogers, author of the *Manual of Coaching*, was a Philadelphian of wealth and of social prominence; he was also enlightened. [*See note, page 286.*] In commissioning this painting he wanted a work of art, not a trophy of leisure-class activity, and Eakins presented him a controlled work in a plain, varnished frame. Rogers liked it and took it to Europe with him. Too small, too honest in its portraits to give comfort to a class, this masterpiece uses the old "facts" of sunlight and time to achieve a psychological and a sociological intensity unique among Eakins' out-of-door scenes.

Scenes painted along the Delaware River a few years later lack this kind of intellectual scrutiny, and again, as in the waterscapes of the early seventies

30. THE FAIRMAN ROGERS FOUR-IN-HAND
1879. 24 x 36. Collection of the Philadelphia Museum of Art.

31. SHAD FISHING AT GLOUCESTER ON THE DELAWARE
1881. 12½ x 18¼. Collection of the Philadelphia Museum of Art.

32. MENDING THE NET
1881. 32 x 45. Collection of the Philadelphia Museum of Art.

33. MENDING THE NET (DETAIL)

their calm precedes the coming of storm in Eakins' history. In the 1881 *Shad Fishing at Gloucester on the Delaware (Figure 31)*, a Sunday group of four well-dressed people, including Benjamin Eakins and one of his daughters, watches a group of Negro fishermen taking up the net into the boat at the right. In the play of sunlight upon the figures each is solidly realized though no individual emerges from the painting, and none is meant to. The mood is subdued and the quest for psychological meaning loses itself in the distance between the unseen painter, the spectator, and the line of men at work. The quiet poetry of sunlight absorbs the painter. [*See note, page 286.*]

A year later the individualized human figure returned to prominence (though its place was still muted, still undramatized) in the greatest masterpiece among these riverside scenes. *Mending the Net (Figure 32)* is the study of a Sunday morning, of the easy postures of the half-dozen men at work on the net, the older man approaching with his basket, the children watching and trying to join the activity, the idler in jacket and straw hat reading his paper on the bench at the right. The quiet isolation of the group on the skyline is very moving in some mysterious way not characteristic of a simple objective realism *(Figure 33)*. The piled lumber and the blighted tree above it particularize place; the tree itself is an evocative symbol of change in a suspended moment. The painting is in part a response to the imperishable hanging light of an early summer morning. We observe that the men engaged in communal work are caught up in personal isolation, in what amounts to a state of trance, and once more the isolated, meditative moment takes hold of us inevitably, unexpectedly. The eye, the hand, the consciousness of a great painter are at work here.

Landscapes painted by Americans of the nineteenth century commonly associated grandeur of effect with size. Eakins was temperamentally and intellectually incapable of aiming at the effects sought by the great cow painters or by the romantically inspired. His vision continued to express itself through the restraints characteristic of him, and his landscapes remained, in opposition to the fashion, controlled responses to mood. The painter's consciousness dominated their spaces, creating a range of effects, low-keyed, infinitely diverse, and essentially apart from the large public tensions in the man's life.

William Rush Carving His Allegorical Figure of the Schuylkill River (1877) *(Figure 34)* one of whose purposes was to evoke the atmosphere of an earlier time, reflects in its way some of the tensions and restraints under which

34. WILLIAM RUSH CARVING HIS ALLEGORICAL FIGURE OF THE SCHUYLKILL RIVER

1877. 20⅛ x 26⅛. Collection of the Philadelphia Museum of Art.

Eakins had to work. It shows William Rush in his studio sculpting a draped figure and using as his model a young woman posing in the nude. She stands in the foreground of the studio but has her back decently to the spectator. A chaperone sits knitting at the right.

In a statement written to accompany the painting, Eakins appealed to the Philadelphian's concern for tradition and to his love for antiquities of any sort in order to establish the respectability of a model's posing in the nude. The appearance of a nude in a finished painting was bound to evoke hostile comment and his statement was meant to anticipate it. An "esteemed merchant" of the early nineteenth century had permitted his daughter to pose for William Rush who carved the waterworks statues Philadelphia knew and found irreproachable. "Rush was a personal friend of Washington, and served in the Revolution," Eakins wrote, and he painted a Rush figure of Washington in the background. The antiques and icons of that studio were meant to guarantee respectability.

Eakins' painting transcended the rhetorical concerns forced upon him. In the light cast upon her the model lives fully, sensuously, with an identity and a beauty unequalled in American painting. She is the painting's life, created out of Eakins' full depth of response to the human figure. In an earlier study the model was heavier; Eakins has idealized her, but it is an idealization close to anatomical reality, and neither academic nor sentimental.

Barker found the painting "a masterpiece of firm construction and delicately tapestried color with which a mind of Quaker restraint might parallel the richer sensuousness of the Venetians. The model is seen from the back as she faces into the studio toward the sculptor at work beyond, while the same slanting light that eloquently reveals the structural subtleties of flesh and bone delineates with equal eloquence the dress folds on the woman seated alongside and the exquisite disorder of discarded clothes piled upon the foreground chair. In textures of flesh and cloth, in a tone where shadow is only a little less luminous than light, Eakins set down with a final beauty the austere sensuousness which vitalized his lofty intelligence." It is an intelligence whose romantic quality — felt in the return to the past, in the use of shadow, and in the treatment of body — is very much in tension with the classical restraints of the craftsman.

Yet it is possible to feel that in seeking so carefully to avoid offense — and one measure of the purely social restraints felt and self-imposed is the size of the painting — he lost some of the force which might have attached to the mystery. What he did not lose, a remarkable feat given the diverse motives that moved him, was his absolute sense of atmosphere, of the most restrained sense of romantic wonder grounded in fact, but taking its light from a human body. [*See note, page 286.*]

In the life-sized *Crucifixion* (1880) *(Figure 35)* he had greater scope for the treatment of body. He used his pupil, John Laurie Wallace, for his model, strapping him to a cross on the roof beneath his fourth-floor studio to observe the strain upon muscles and tendons. The painting, like the *Christ Crucified* of Velásquez, is an unemotional rendering of the subject, an attempt to say something of spirit through what has been done to that body so strikingly isolated against the cold gray-blue sky. [*See note, page 286.*] Is there more understanding of the physical agony — in the observation of chest and arms, of the face in shadow beneath the crown of thorns, and of the stiffened fingers of the nailed hands — than there is feeling? The fervor comes through strangely in the calligraphy of the legend nailed to the cross.

He painted a number of other nudes in the early eighties using his sister's children as models at their farm in Avondale, Pennsylvania. He photographed the Crowell children in the nude and used the photographs for his studies, yet the differences between the photographs and the paintings underline that between the more or less objective camera eye and the artist's vision. *Arcadia (Figure 36)*, painted in 1883, has a poignant effect which his photographs of nudes in similar positions do not suggest. In the foreground of this free landscape a young girl listens to two boys playing the pipes of Pan. There is an effect of yearning, of deep personal feeling attaching to the painting — and, it may be, something unsatisfactory in the attitudes of the figures, all turned away from the spectator, types of youth, of childhood, without identities, caught up in dream. Behind his failure to finish this painting or any of the other arcadian studies is the repressive force of a civilization which could approve this use of the imagination no more than it might the Whitmanesque, or the Michelangelesque, for that matter. There was no place for an Arcadia of nudes in the imagination of a Philadelphian, and none certainly for the freedoms or the scope of a *Battle of Cascine*.

In the attempt to discover other reasonable uses for the nude, and to legitimize new subject matter, new themes, and new effects in American painting, Eakins did in fact choose a vaguely Michelangelesque theme when, in 1883, he painted *The Swimming Hole (Figure 37)*. It was a painting, F. O. Matthiessen felt, no less daring than a Whitman poem in what it attempted, its portrait of a group of naked men seen against a summer landscape; he was

35. THE CRUCIFIXION
1880. 96 x 54. Collection of the Philadelphia Museum of Art.

36. ARCADIA
1883. 38¾ x 45. Adelaide Milton de Groot.

37. THE SWIMMING HOLE
1883. 27 x 36. Collection of the Fort Worth Art Association.

38. THE PATHETIC SONG

1881. 45½ x 32½. In the Collection of The Corcoran Gallery of Art.

reminded of Whitman's "Twenty-Eight Young Men Bathe by the Shore."

The figures of *The Swimming Hole* yield to time as they do to sunlight and water, fixed there in a rhythmical pyramid, enveloped by time as they are by space. Oliver Larkin remarked upon the "splendid corporeality of a Signorelli figure" in the man standing on the rock at the apex of the pyramid, and upon the painting's rare qualities of atmosphere and design: "Out of the reclining, the leaning, the swinging of the six bodies, Eakins created a rhythm in space as well as a frontal pattern upward to the crowning figure and swiftly down to the river. Within the depth given by his water, his mass of projecting rock, and the wooded bank beyond he gave his bodies an air-surrounded solidity that had seldom been seen in America." The pyramidal form gives the painting its certain small monumental quality, the sense of permanence attaching to the casual event.

Eakins prepared wax models for the nude figures and again worked from a photograph in painting *The Swimming Hole,* yet one may object to the reminders of the studio in those poses only by refusing to see in them a psychological expressiveness achievable by no other artist at that time, or by failing to respond to the certainty with which the total work evokes its mood, its lyricism, its sense of pagan ease. There is more valid reason for regret. Despite his absolute mastery of the human figure, Eakins could not permit himself to paint a male figure with his genitals showing. The painting's subject, strangely enough, had been commissioned by Edward Horner Coates, Director of the Pennsylvania Academy at the time. Faced with as much nudity as he found there, that gentleman chose, instead, to purchase *The Pathetic Song (Figure 38).* Eakins, swimming at the right, was in his fortieth year when he painted *The Swimming Hole,* but this "brave and exceptional attempt by an American to treat the heroic theme of naked men in a natural setting" was to find no further expression in his work.

COATES was not entirely foolish in his choice. *The Pathetic Song,* completed some two years before, was to be one of the most moving statements of Eakins' attachment to the values of the community he knew, a working out of the meanings implied five years before by *The Chess Players (Figure 27).* It is the painter's response to the communal moment, to the three absorbed performers in a musical recital that helps to set this work apart from so many like it in the nineteenth century. The effect is inseparable from a form implying permanence, an unmoving trancelike state, and a theme and subject that suggest the transitory, the mutable.

Again he fixes the moment in a triangular grouping of figures. Light falls from the left upon the singer, her blue-gray dress, her face, throat, and ear, and upon the head and hands of the cellist. In the darker background Susan Macdowell, the pianist, a silent choric figure, absorbs and reflects the scene's mood. The painting focuses upon the lovely vitality of the young woman singing, moves backward into its shadows, then out from the depth of Susan Macdowell's response, to the cellist, the cello barely touched with light, upward to the face of the singer. It is not easy to think of an interior scene in which Eakins is more subtly and more forcefully the master of atmosphere, of effect, and of a significance beyond what he so simply and movingly represents. He believes in the highly civilized social order which can produce these sensitive people. In their fleeting communal moment they assert the immemorial value of simple human responsiveness. It is their world that held Eakins in Philadelphia, not the society of *The Fairman Rogers Four-in-Hand (Figure 30)*. In the five years since the painting of *The Chess Players* he had discovered something like the proper magnitude for the affection he felt for his immediate world, for the scale of *The Pathetic Song* is fully and precisely expressive of the current of deep restrained feeling that animates it.

Four years and a profound emotional distance separate *The Pathetic Song* from the work that climaxes the period, marking the end of this crucial era for Eakins. In 1884 he had married Susan Hannah Macdowell and in 1885 he painted her portrait *(Figure 39)*, a work so absolutely honest and so daring in its use of color, form and light to achieve its restrained and understated effects that it could have been painted only by a great master. [*See note, page 286.*] Susan Eakins, her head slightly inclined, looks out directly at the spectator in a glance simultaneously inquiring and understanding, a scrutiny implying both self-recognition and objective judgment, self-deprecation and a knowledge of reality. The lady is burdened by her consciousness, by a head too large for a body seemingly drained of vitality. Yet in her eyes and mouth, and in the flexed, open left hand, sensitive, but surprisingly strong, character and individuality reveal themselves. (Our attention moves from Susan Eakins' eyes to the hand over the Japanese picture book; he discovers the soul in eyes and hands.) The lady has the capacity to contemplate life's finite possibilities directly, knowingly. Eakins has advanced from the portrait of Katherine, where character was plainly an unprotesting product of environment, to a vision of a woman forcefully conscious of its coercive force. Beneath this large meaning are more personal ones.

39. PORTRAIT OF A LADY WITH A SETTER DOG
1885. 30 x 23. The Metropolitan Museum of Art, Fletcher Fund, 1923.

The kitten in Katherine's lap becomes the setter at Susan's feet and in the dog Harry's heavy, flattened attention there may be a parody of Susan's scrutiny, an unaccustomed irony. The lady with a setter dog, wearing a blue dress and red slippers, in a room with a curtain, a secretary and an oriental rug, is the artist's wife in his studio. There are paintings on the wall, the relief called *Arcadia* at the right, and on the wall, left, is one of his studies of women, perhaps of Margaret, her head bent in reflection, or over some task. Caught up between his profound personal response to his wife as individual and his recognition of larger meanings, Eakins shaped a work as truthful in revealing his personal effect upon his wife as it is in discovering her response to an era and to a milieu. No other American artist of the time was capable of psychological effects such as this, and none could bring color and light like this to the service of a vision so profound, so compassionate and so lacking in the sentimental. In the *Portrait of a Lady with a Setter Dog* Eakins arrived, after whatever discoveries and disillusions, after whatever evasions and returns, however willingly or unwillingly, at one of the important centers of his consciousness.

SUSAN EAKINS first saw her future husband, in the middle seventies, seated on a table at the Haseltine Galleries where *The Gross Clinic* was being exhibited. She studied with him at the Pennsylvania Academy and he thought her one of his best students. She was Katherine Crowell's age, twenty-seven, when Katherine Crowell died, thirty when Margaret Eakins died, thirty-two when she married Eakins in 1884. Her face in the *Portrait* of 1885 measures some of the tensions of that period. A year later her husband was forced to resign his position at the Pennsylvania Academy.

7

The human body is itself the
richest and raciest phrase book.
— Bronson Alcott

IN 1882 a young woman of fervent conviction wrote a letter to J. L. Claghorn, President of the Pennsylvania Academy, to warn of insidious threats to public morality in that institution. This letter, primitive in its sentiments to be sure, is, in its way, a masterpiece. It expresses the heat of its outrage with a ladylike sincerity that is undeniable, and defines the high moral atmosphere in which Eakins and the new Academy attempted to breathe and to live. As a literary work it may require a word or two of analysis. It begins with a modest exordium, and ends with an impassioned peroration before its ladylike return to a tone of reason. It grounds its rhetorical appeals (to church, to religion) in an unassailable definition of Art, and then rapidly moves to its sustained view of the corruptive forces and horrors of nudity. In two staccato paragraphs the moral issues are brought ever more clearly into focus; the next two by their metaphorical reference ("Does it pay?") bring the letter first to a heat, then to its nicely incoherent ecstasy in the vision of the Heavenly Father.

West Philadelphia
April 11th, 1882

Mr. J. L. Claghorn,
Dear Sir,

I know you will be surprised and perhaps astonished at the courage of a lady to address the "President of the Academy of Fine Arts" in reference to a subject which just at this time seems to be so popular and to which the President and Directors of the Academy are giving their earnest support and aid. This is an age of progress I know, and especially of great improvements in Arts and Sciences, and I acknowledge that every effort should be made and sustained with enthusiasm that promotes true Art. By *true Art* I mean, the Art that enobles and purifies the mind, elevates the whole intellect, increases the love of the beautiful, and as nothing can be beautiful that is not pure and holy, that so elevates humanity that it becomes better fit to enjoy that purity and holiness, that belongs to immortality. Now I appeal to you as a Christian gentleman, educated amidst the pure and holy teaching of our beloved Church, and where the exortations to purity of mind and body were amongst your earliest *home* teachings, to consider for a moment the effect of the teaching of the Academy, on the young and sensitive minds of both the male and female students. I allude to the Life Class studies, and I know where of I speak. Would you be willing to take a young daughter of your own into the Academy Life Class, to the study of the *nude figure* of a woman, whom you would shudder to have sit in your parlor clothed and converse with your daughter? Would you be willing to sit there with your daughter, or know she was sitting there with a dozen others, *studying* a nude figure, while the professor walked around criticising that nudity, as to her *roundness in this part,* and swell of the muscles in another? That daughter at home had been shielded from every thought that might lead her young mind from the most rigid chastity. Her mother had never allowed her to see her young naked brothers, hardly her sisters after their babyhood and yet at the age of eighteen, or nineteen, for the culture of *high Art,* she had entered a class where both *male* and female figures stood before her in their horrid nakedness. This is no imaginary picture. I know at this time two young ladies of culture, refined families, enthusiastic students of painting, whose parents, after earnest entreaties of patrons of Art and assurances that Art could *only be studied* successfully BY ENTERING such a class, consented, with the assurance from their daughters that if they found the study as improper as their parents feared they would desist. They entered, and from their own lips I heard the statement of the terrible shock to their feelings *at first,* how they trembled when the professor came, one stating she thought she should faint. Her fellow students, who had been in the class for some time, assured her that she would soon *get over that,* and not mind it at all! She persevered, and now "don't mind seeing a naked man or woman in the least." She has learned to consider it the only road to *high Art,* and has become so interested she never sees a fine looking person without thinking what a fine *nude study* they would make! What has become of her *womanly* refinement and delicacy?

Do you wonder why so many art students are unbelievers, even infidels? Why there is often so much looseness of morals among the young men? Is there anything so effective in awakening licentiousness as this daily and *nightly* study of woman's nudity! Can it be helped! Can Christian men, members of the church, deliberately aid in demoralizing the young in this manner and not be guilty!

There is not a young woman who has been a member of the life class for any length of time, but has become more or less coarse in manner and word. I have been thrown with them and know of what I speak. A young gentleman, a very promising artist, who studied at the Academy for a time, does not hesitate to say that it is *impossible* to study in the life class and retain your *purity of thought!*

Now, Mr. Claghorn, does this pay! Does it pay, for a young lady of a refined, godly household to be urged as the only way of obtaining a knowledge of true Art, to enter a class where every feeling of *maidenly* delicacy is violated, where she becomes so hardened to indelicate sights and words, so familiar with the persons of degraded women and the sight of nude males, that *no possible* art can restore her lost treasure of *chaste and delicate thoughts!* There is no use in saying that she must look upon the study as she would that of a wooden figure! That is an *utter impossibility*. Living, moving flesh and blood, is not, cannot, be studied thus. The stifling heat of the room, adds to the excitement, and what might be a cool unimpassioned study in a room at 35 degrees, at 85 degrees or even higher is dreadful.

Then with this dreadful exposure of body and mind, not one in a dozen could make a respectable *draped* figure. Spending two years in life study of *flesh color*, that a decent artist would never need, and then have to begin over again for the draped figure. Where is the elevating enobling influence of the beautiful art of painting in these studies? The study of the beautiful in landscape and draped figures, and the exquisitely beautiful in the flowers that the Heavenly Father has decked and beautified the world with, is ignored, sneered at, and that only made the grand object of the ambition of the student of Art, that comes unholy thoughts with it, that the Heavenly Father Himself covered from the sight of his fallen children.

Pray excuse this liberty in writing to you but I have been made to feel that the subject is one of such vital importance to the morals of our young students I could not refrain.

Very truly yours,
R. S.

THE Pennsylvania Academy of Fine Arts was, in the early part of the nineteenth century, a dome-roofed rotunda fifty feet in diameter with light in the center, a leaking roof and a rotting floor. Students copied casts from the antique there, but visitors seldom broke the solitude. Reading John Sartain's *Reminiscences* of that time one gathers that it was considered virtually inaccessible in its location on Chestnut Street beyond Tenth. The decayed roof was eventually replaced with slate but a fire destroyed the collection of casts; substitutes for these were not found for a dozen years.

In 1868 John Sartain conceived a plan for establishing a proper art school at the Pennsylvania Academy — in part, at least, to aid his partially paralyzed friend, Christian Schussele, who could teach at the school when he became unable to paint. Eakins began to teach at the Academy at 1876, and when Schussele died in 1879 he became its professor of drawing and painting. [*See note, page 286.*] As professor, and later as Director of Instruction, he made it the best school of its kind in the country. In doing so he worked against the deepest instincts of its directors.

That grand exotic structure designed by Frank Furness at Broad and Cherry streets, the new Academy, was an act of faith promulgated and paid for by Philadelphia's elect. They had made money during the Civil War in ways that may or may not have reflected their love of God and Country, and now they wished to build a temple to their culture and to the truth that had eluded them during the war years and during the brilliant youth of the Gilded Age. They wanted a fortress where True Art might be kept pure, undirtied, uncontaminated by the world as they had known it, an Academy where they might send their daughters if need be, a safe place where girls might be kept until they married, a bank in which their social and aesthetic pretensions might draw interest.

Eakins came to the Academy with other ideas about the function of its school. He did not mean to attack the determined complacency of the Academy's directors. He meant simply to teach painting as he had come to feel it had to be taught.

The schools of the Pennsylvania Academy of Fine Arts, Fairman Rogers wrote, explaining Eakins' views, "are supported in the interest of those who intend to become professional artists. . . . The system pursued is not that best adapted to the teaching of drawing as an accomplishment, or to cultivating tastes among amateurs." The schools assumed that broad culture would be attained by students before and after their period at the Academy, and admitted, in this sense, that its art instruction was "somewhat narrow." But its course of study, Rogers believed, was more thorough than that of any existing school. Its basis was not the antique cast, but the nude human figure.

No school in America dared use the nude model in mid-century America. [*See note, page 287.*] To paint a nude in America, however academic or sentimental, had always been to invite social disaster. The Puritan response was consistent with a Manichaeanism that located evil in material reality, in body. A genteel culture devotes itself to the task of disguising or ignoring reality; the Academy was meant to exclude it. All sin is through body, and body must be decently clothed. If body was also life, it was far better not to be reminded of it while one was earnestly attempting to survive under the old agricultural dispensation, or earnestly trying to control life in the new time of science and industry.

Eakins went in resolute search of models. In his teaching he sought to make the use of the nude more respectable than it had been by advertising for girls of good family to pose for the students. They might be chaperoned by their mothers. Students might also pose for one another, though not in mixed classes. Before that students had found models in houses of prostitution, and Eakins had not found those women beautiful.

He also taught human and equine anatomy using human cadavers and the bodies of horses. Sometimes he found dissection no less unpleasant than his students did, but he was convinced that truth and a deeper understanding of beauty lay through that sort of knowledge of body. Later he came to think that he had spent too much time in the study of anatomy; but in that early vigorous period of his teaching something in the climate of the century and in his own experience compelled him to use science in the service of art. It was a protection, a justification.

If most of his students respected him, few had the wideness of culture that he had hopefully posited to fully appreciate what he was attempting to do and there were undercurrents of restlessness among them that communicated themselves to society.

The tenure of Thomas Eakins at the Academy was dependent upon the presence of Fairman Rogers, who thought much as he did. Rogers was director of the Academy's Board of Trustees, but he was also an enlightened friend who understood and appreciated Eakins' genius. He was an engineer, a dilettante of art and of scientific inquiry, and an amateur of some eminence of the art and science of coaching. He was a member of the National Academy of Sciences, and of the American Philosophical Society. He had money and an unassailable social position. He had been commander of the 1st Troop of the Philadelphia City Cavalry and Member of the Board of Trustees at the University of Pennsylvania. By 1883, at the age of fifty, this good urbane man, ready to defend Eakins upon any occasion (he quieted the offended who objected when students flung the body of a horse down the stairwell during a Masonic dinner), was also ready to quit Philadelphia. His resignation from the Academy left Eakins with no weapon but his integrity.

When Eakins removed the loincloth from the male model in 1886, he was performing an act of ritual, an immolation. The directors of the Academy were equally ready to perform their own role. The protests of his loyal students were of no help to him: the directors cast him out. And they made their voice heard in an editorial explaining their spiritual responsibilities. "The life school of the Academy is a benefaction established by the directors for the good of the students, and absolutely under the directors' control. It is their school and nobody's else." [*See note, page 287.*]

THOMAS ANSHUTZ succeeded Eakins at the Pennsylvania Academy. He stayed on to toady to the board of directors and to furtively echo the master. If he had learned anything from Eakins, it was not his integrity and not the ability to paint a great picture. In the 1890's he felt the need of instruction, and he went to Paris where he chose Bouguereau and Doucet as his masters. He had neither Eakins' intelligence nor his moral sense, and so was able to stay at the Academy beyond the time of John Sloan, and indeed to succeed William Merritt Chase as its head in 1909. Though Sloan and Anshutz later became friends, Sloan left the Academy in 1903 when Anshutz admonished him for drawing from the antique during a life class. Thus are changes wrought on an old theme.

A gallery in New York, scratching at thin soil, attempted to revive Anshutz in 1963. In a typical portrait of this master of the banal the arm of a woman, usually the right, is raised and the hand is lost behind the head, or the fingers are fixed to suggest thought or tension. The common mood of these women is ennui; for the most part they are coy and sexless. Nor is this merely a reflection of his material. Nothing in Anshutz, no understanding of form, no use of color or of shadow reveals anything but a prosaic mind. His portraits are somber and without depth; large and without monumentality. He pretends to intellectual and moral qualities that he does not have. Anshutz was a board-of-directors' man, acceptable to the public. The portentous scowl of his self-portrait arrests one for a moment, but that scowl is empty, that brooding focused on nothing, unless it is upon the path he had chosen. [*See note, page 287.*]

8

THERE is a great pity in the spectacle of Eakins, this man of forty-three grown heavy but still physically powerful, his quiet high voice a token of his vulnerability, now immobile and uncertain. With no mask and no cunning he had tried to fill the incompatible roles of director of a public institution and of existential man, attempting to impose his absolute morality upon the institution. His honesty, in the narrowest and most basic sense his recognition of the psychological, biological and temporal realities beneath the social appearance, had asserted itself in a civilization obsessively concerned to maintain that appearance, and to insist upon it as the only significant reality. He could not chart the official course, and when he ran aground, shipwrecked on the shoals of Philadelphia's genteel consciousness, he saw what he had always known was there, and yet thought there was some fault in himself.

Bedeviled by incapacity and uncertainty, he went West in 1887 in an attempt to regain vitality. He rode, made notes for landscapes, and returned, childlike, to his beloved city, riding one horse from the railway station, leading another. But he required something other than a temporary retreat from that civilization and other than a flight to a more primitive one. In retrospect it appears that he required contact with someone who had attempted to probe the American experience as honestly as he had. In Eakins' life, temperamental affinities were always of great importance. At some time in 1887 after his return from Dakota, with his friend Talcott Williams, editor of the *Press*, he crossed the Delaware to Camden, where Williams introduced him to Walt Whitman.

As vastly different temperamentally as they were in the practice of their arts, the two men had common ground in their honesty, in their anti-authoritarian impulses, and in their suspicion of official morality and of official art. Whitman's Faustian exuberances, his incantatory catalogs, his loosening of form were expressions of the romantic's attempt to swallow all of life. When we consider the restraints of Eakins' temperament and of his art, his concentration, and his concern for form, it may be difficult to understand how he was moved by *Leaves of Grass* or later by *Democratic Vistas*. The Faustian man and the "grand provincial" differed radically in their kinds of aesthetic sophistication, Whitman's the all inclusive, refusing nothing, Eakins' the more intellectually discriminating, defining the limits of the possible. But Eakins was also moved by Rabelais, and he could accept the priest and the poet as priest in their role as liberators, opposing provincial mores in their attempt to free vision. In Whitman's assault upon the genteel tradition he could read his own history. In his early work he had discovered, in images Whitman himself might have chosen, something like the spirit of the poet's romanticism. If he could not identify himself with every form of American life, he had full experience of that attempt to enter the spirit of his subject which is the key to his power. Never the painter of ideal democracy, unable to conceive anything like a Whitmanesque abstraction in his work, Eakins nevertheless found himself expressing an idealism in almost everything he painted, through the communicated force of his conviction that beauty as well as the vitality of "big painting" could be achieved by trusting to vision grounded in one's deepest perceptions, unclouded by the necessities of official art.

Official art, for one thing, did not permit any profound expression of sexuality in its works, the sort of expression Eakins achieved intuitively, an intuition grounded, to be sure, in all his intellectual training. "Any one brought up among Puritans knew that sex was sin," Henry Adams was to remark of this period. Like James, Adams appears to have been ignorant of Eakins' work, and so when he turned to art in American civilization to find some equivalent of the Virgin who might give power to creativity, energy to the American mind, "asking himself whether he knew of any American artist who had ever insisted on the power of sex, as every classic had always done, he could only think of Walt Whitman. . . . American art, like the American language and the American education was as far as possible sexless. Society regarded this victory over sex as its greatest triumph." Adams named Saint-Gaudens as the most sympathetic "of all the American artists who gave to American art whatever life it breathed in the seventies." Yet Saint-Gaudens precisely lacks that quality of penetrating sexual insight which was habitual to Eakins' vision.

Responsive to Whitman's call for sexual liberation and sexual honesty, he was no less so to the poet as prophet and moralist surveying his time. Whitman had published *Democratic Vistas* in 1870, the year of Eakins' return from Europe. The young Philadelphian had not been ready for its message then, but experience ripened him for it. By 1887 the perceptions expressed in it formed another bond between him and Whitman. "Society in these States is canker'd, crude, superstitious and rotten," Whitman had written. "Moral conscience seems to me either entirely lacking, or seriously enfeebled or ingrown." In attacking the conditions of post Civil War America, Whitman made his call for a literature which would express "a religious and moral character . . . beneath the political and productive and intellectual bases of the states." Although he seems to have despaired of painting performing any such role because it was no longer "a medium of the intellect," he sought in it something very much like that emotionally responsive and yet profoundly intellectual art Eakins was to shape. More conscious perhaps of the difficulties of such an art than Emerson was, Whitman is no less enthusiastic in ordering the attack: "Yet is there an immortal courage and prophecy in every sane soul that cannot, must not, under any circumstances, capitulate. *Vive* the attack — the perennial assault! *Vive* the unpopular cause — the spirit that audaciously aims, the never abandoned efforts." Addressing the great man to come directly, he asks, "Thought you greatness was to ripen for you like a pear? If you would have greatness know that you must conquer it through ages, centuries — must pay for it with a proportionate price." Eakins may or may not have read this exhortation; but he was encouraged by the man who had refused to yield before his own experience of misunderstanding and hostility, and he carried out his own program by the same sort of instinct.

Whitman's understanding of Eakins and his fidelity to him showed themselves whenever he felt called upon to defend him or his art. At their first meeting, Whitman's impression was of a man "careless, negligent, indifferent . . . negative in quality, manner, intuition," but he came rapidly to understand Eakins' inwardness. If he had "no parlor gallantries," he was not lacking in the "graces of friendship" and if others found him "uncouth, unchary, boorish," Whitman thought him no more so than himself. The social graces took their place in the ordering of a man's life, perhaps fourth place for an Eakins, said Whitman.

When Eakins completed the portrait of him, Whitman's first impression was again not positive. He did not find it pleasant. But he came around to feeling the profundity of its insight. "My own impression summed up is, that the painting is a genuine piece of work . . . a quite extraordinary piece of work: may one day be considered even a great production . . . Eakins is not the man to be choked off by a few unripe or overripe dissenters." Few of Whitman's visitors liked the portrait. Among the dissenters were John Burroughs, who felt that it had "defects of tone," and Herbert Gilchrist, who objected to Eakins' "tortuous methods." Gilchrist told Whitman that the portrait falsified him and was "a dangerous picture to make current." Whitman thereupon heaped his scorn upon Gilchrist:

Herbert is in the London swim — likes the swell crowd — endorsing its codes, sharing its worships, sailing by its beacon. He belongs with the Royal Academy Nabobs: the Sir Frederick Leighton kind of reigning Monarchs (that's him, ain't it?), adept (Ah! a miraculously skilled man) in technique, style, traditions, a great man according to existing rules . . . Herbert is in with that class, is inbred with its interests, crochets, idiocrities — not one of them, of the whole London crowd, . . . direct. . . . How could they appreciate Eakins, who breaks utterly from the old, the outworn, the merely traditional? Then we must remember that the Eakins picture is severe — keeps close to nature — slurs nothing — faces the worst as well as the best. . . .

The Gilchrist portrait of Whitman is *art-officiel*, bland and passionless. [*See note, page 289.*] Whitman called it "the parlor Whitman." The poet, a benign icon for the Philistine, is seated in his shaggy tweeds, full faced, his legs crossed, his right hand holding a pencil and resting on a tablet. The poet's glance is the quizzical yet reassuring look of established wisdom.

Herbert is determined to make me the conventional, proper old man: his picture is very benevolent, to be sure: but the Walt Whitman of that picture lacks guts. . . . The very worst place in the world to put Herbert's picture would be right next to Eakins. It would be sure death.

Another portrait of Whitman, once well known, was painted by John W. Alexander whose *The Spirit of Pittsburgh* was for a time famous as America's most expensive painting. The genteel tradition, speaking through the painter, a master of the incorporeal and the unsubstantial, produced the Spirit, a knight in armor, floating benevolently above the pleasant landscape. Alexan-

40. SKETCH FOR PORTRAIT OF WALT WHITMAN
1887. 5¼ x 5¼. Museum of Fine Arts, Boston (Helen and Alice Colburn Fund).

41. WALT WHITMAN
1887-1888. 30 x 24. The Pennsylvania Academy of the Fine Arts.

der's Whitman was a vaporous deification of the poet. Years after it was painted Walter Pach spoke indignantly of its "gaseous silhouette." Horace Traubel reacted hostilely to the "pinched and formalized Whitman," but the portrait was generally admired by the American public at the Metropolitan Museum. "I liked to have Alexander here," said Whitman; "he is the right stuff for a man though I am not sure he is the right stuff for a painter." In speaking of Alexander Whitman made the well-known remark about Eakins that, taken out of context, is a powerful half-truth. "Tom Eakins could give Alexander a lot of extra room and yet beat him at the game. Eakins is not a painter, he is a force. Alexander is a painter."

During the celebration of his seventy-second birthday, Whitman called upon Eakins to speak.

W: And Eakins — What of Tom Eakins. He is here. Haven't you something to say to us Eakins?

E: I am not a speaker.

W: So much the better — you are more likely to say something.

Forced to adopt the social graces, Eakins spoke of his difficulty in painting the "picture of Mr. Whitman. I began in the usual way, but soon found that the ordinary methods wouldn't do — that technique, rules and traditions would have to be thrown aside; that before all else, he was to be treated as a man, whatever became of what are commonly called the principles of art."

His remarks were more than mere parlor gallantries; they testify to an artist's not infrequent sense of incapacity before a demanding subject, before that moment of discovery and invention when his knowledge and his craft may find themselves at the service of deeper intuitions. The small sketch for the portrait *(Figure 40)* communicates the spontaneous force of this intuition, the astonishing immediacy of Eakins' reaction to the man. It is the head of a physically wasted old man in whom one feels the quality of exceptional life — the spirit of a seer, a visionary, a Homer, the fragile husk barely enveloping that life, the eyes closed, the left eye caught in shadow, the light striking the right side of the head, the whole evoking a sense of twilight, of the rapid movement toward life's dissolution, and the most moving effect of great pity.

The finished portrait *(Figure 41)* has an entirely different effect. Confronted by a personality who might be understood through no formula for character, Eakins "put aside the rules" and discovered something very like an enigma. There is little agreement about the impression it produces. Is it "slightly leering" as Lewis Mumford felt? Is it glum? "If I thought it would finally look glum I would hate it," said Whitman. Does it err on the side of the flesh, as both Traubel and Whitman occasionally thought? "All the features of Whitman's face suggest inception and amplitude," said Traubel. "Hence the failure of Alexander to make of his pinched and formalized Whitman anything which can have value. Hence the explanation why Eakins, in that glorious head . . . expressed by so many hints the life of the man."

". . . by so many hints, the life of the man." Whitman's force was in his consciousness not in his paralyzed and wasting body, and Eakins attacked the head directly. But in the head itself he can say enough about the adventure of this consciousness, caught in body, bearing its weight of mortality through its own history and revealing itself in this moment. The strength of the portrait cannot be suggested by a reproduction. The *Whitman* communicates as much through the handling of paint itself as any portrait by Eakins does. He did not throw aside "techniques, rules and traditions" but made them organic to his vision. Whitman's eyes (are they shrewd? hurt?) are set in the flesh of an old man's face, flushed old flesh. Whitman and Traubel felt it: the submergence of spirit in the biological man. What time and the world have done to Whitman are clear enough if we look for the signs. Shoulder, arm, chest, and the gut beneath his vest fill half the portrait — but they are all dominated by that powerful head whose submerged spirit is its life. The painting is a massive yet deeply searching confrontation of the poet's consciousness. The head stands out against the dark brown background, the brush marking the formidable inwardness, the head smiling or weeping, monumental, heroic, enduring. [*See note, page 289.*]

9

"There is no tyranny more exacting or despotic than that exercised by the conventionalities which govern our living. . . . Beyond all contradiction, the behests of convention are vastly more influential in governing public conduct than any argument drawn from the teachings of structure and function."

—D. Hayes Agnew, M.D., on "The Relation of Social Life to Surgical Disease"

EAKINS visited Whitman in Camden over a period of four and a half years, a fairly productive time with more than one mark of the poet upon it. It was not merely that Whitman believed in him, but that Whitman's affirmations were grounded in his own deep experience of alienation, and in his equally profound knowledge of the meaning of mortality. His central work of this period, *The Agnew Clinic* (1889) was a titanic physical and psychic effort for Eakins, a celebration, in effect, of the triumph of mortal life through the efforts of a community of men led by another inspired physician. When it was completed it was received by the larger public as hostilely as *The Gross Clinic* had been. The relative importance of this second public rejection of a major work in finally limiting Eakins' range and the future uses of his imagination can hardly be overstated.

Yet though he completed little else in that year, he was able to go on, painting friends mostly, and students who interested him at the Art Students League. The effect of each work was still very much determined by his response to the sitter, though certain kinds of responses tended to recur. A current of romanticism flowed strongly in a number of portraits of men—reminiscent of the Whitman interpretation—while in several of older men, more realistic in the ordinary sense, of William Macdowell *(Figures 77-80)*, of George Fetter *(Figure 50)*, and of Henry Rowland

(Figure 51), he achieved as much as he ever had in the way of psychological understanding and sheer human statement, pointing the way to the shape of his vision in those to come. In the portraits of women, he became ever more intensely and meaningfully involved with the problem of beauty, discovering it in color and design which, seemingly uninventive, are yet inimitable, as well as through psychological insight and the scrutiny of expression and gesture. He sought it not through the stereotyped idealizations of physical beauty common to the period but through his response to the woman herself: that response was frequently considered too objective and so too harsh in his time, but it is apparent today that a portrait was always a distinctly personal expression, and more frequently admiring than critical. He appeared ever more consciously concerned with the significance of entire lifetimes and we find him moving beyond the psychology of character to a larger questioning of the meaning of individual existence. Finally, the spirit of Whitman was in much of this work. It showed itself as the rediscovery of strong elements in his own nature, in affirmations inherent in the discovery of beauty and meaning in images felt to be distasteful and distressing by an audience bred in the genteel tradition.

When they offered him seven hundred fifty dollars for the portrait of Dr. D. Hayes Agnew, their retiring professor of surgery, the graduating class of 1889 at the University of Pennsylvania Medical School demonstrated that the public view of the artist was not entirely unanimous. *The Gross Clinic*, on view at the Jefferson Medical College since it had been bought for two hundred dollars in 1878, had found a certain favor among men not threatened by the sight of blood or by a bare buttock. Nor were medical students likely to feel that ineradicable disgrace attached to a teacher who had been dismissed from his position at the Academy because he had taken the loincloth from a male model before a mixed audience of students.

Eakins and Dr. Agnew were alike in their devotion to principle, though they differed vastly in their views of propriety. In May 1871, Dr. Agnew had resigned from the staff of Attending Surgeons at the Pennsylvania Hospital after refusing the request of its Board of Managers to lecture to the students of the Women's Medical College. "A modest-minded physician would naturally shrink" from the task of exposing young women, perhaps seventeen or eighteen years old, to the "unpleasant sights and facts" of venereal diseases, his biographer explained. A Philadelphia gentleman first and foremost, Dr. Agnew had found himself momentarily but not irreparably in conflict with the demands of the new science. This strange situation is worth remarking for it is the only known instance in which a gentleman was made to suffer for his defense of the genteel position in Philadelphia. Was science showing itself at last more formidable than outmoded convention? Art was surely a lesser revolutionary force.

Six years after his resignation, Dr. Agnew accepted reelection to the staff of the Pennsylvania Hospital. Although neither his views nor those of the directors had altered he was capable of compromise. When women had the temerity to attend occasional lectures after that, "he interpreted their presence to ignorance of his views on the subject; and, moreover, he was entirely too courteous and kindly in his feelings toward everyone to object to the presence of the women . . . even if they overwhelmed him." This reasonable patriarch "believed that the ideal place for women was at home. . . . Yet he held the sex in great respect and consideration, and did not belittle their powers or capability for work." Thomas Eakins, no feminist himself, could not have disagreed with platitudes so nicely expressing the general wisdom.

For his fee Eakins proposed to paint the entire graduating class along with Dr. Agnew, to paint an Agnew clinic on an even greater scale than the earlier work. In the preliminary three-quarter-length sketch of the isolated figure of Dr. Agnew *(Figure 42)* he produced a portrait whose plain power of statement ranks with any ever painted. Dr. Agnew, poised with the scalpel in his left hand, gestures with his lowered right hand. There is a consciousness of intellectual power and of human dignity in the extraordinary living figure, in the study of intelligence and professional competence joined vitally to feeling and to compassion. In the sculpted nobility of that head there is the best of civilization in late nineteenth-century America.

Eakins worked on the large canvas on the floor of his Chestnut Street studio, painting the students and Dr. Agnew who came in to pose, working steadily for several months, occasionally falling asleep in exhaustion on the floor next to it. *The Agnew Clinic* was conceived, as *The Gross Clinic* had been, out of the passion of sacred awe.

When Eakins had used the contrasting darks and lights in *The Gross Clinic (Figure 22)* to record the operating conditions of the time, he had also used a palette to achieve the dramatic mixture of romantic and realistic effects characteristic of that work. The discovery of the principles of antisepsis, and more specifically, the use of white in the operating rooms, correspond to a changed way of seeing things. In *The Agnew Clinic* (*Figure 43*) solidity and intensity are achieved apart from radical contrasts of tone. The dramatic intensity in the vision of Dr. Gross dominating his clinic by the plain power of will and intellect has given way to the expression of another sort of force.

There is a difference in the men, of course, but that is not all. Though it is in the head of Dr. Agnew that *The Agnew Clinic* finds its most concentrated meaning, that head is not made the focus of light at the apex of a pyramid of human forms as it had been in the earlier painting. *The Gross Clinic* is about eight feet high by six and one-half wide. *The Agnew Clinic*, slightly more than six feet high, is nearly twice that in width, almost thirteen feet. Dr. Agnew is well to the left of the painting's center, his head barely above the level of his assistants. He dominates the work not like the hero of drama but like the hero of epic, by the strength of his more deeply human qualities. Will gives way to qualities of endurance, intellect to an understanding that includes and is not dominated by science. The meaning of the painting does not lie in the figure of the isolated physician rising above mortality, but in the physician communicating his sense of mortality, and participating in it too. The work is bluntly daring in its design, balancing the poised intelligence of Dr. Agnew against the absorbed activity of the operating group, focusing the large human concern of that audience equally upon the doctor, enclosed by the dynamic sweep of the amphitheater, and upon the patient, the woman who has just had a breast removed.

The Agnew Clinic hangs today over the doorway to the University Medical Library; that place ranks high among the settings for an Eakins painting. From the balcony half a floor above the library one stands at the painting's level, about thirty feet away. Here the full power of this work makes itself felt in the very special dominance the figure of Agnew maintains, and in the astonishing life of the operating group. The intense vitality of the surgeon is seen against that background of the postures and faces of the student audience forming their loose attentive community; the teacher is the inspired vessel of the meaning discovered in the woman upon the table. The iron almost brutal force of Dr. Gross is focal to the feeling of that painting; here it is some more communal feeling, something very like compassion. The most moving mirror of that response is the face of Nurse Clymer, the mature Eakins' equivalent for the distressed mother of *The Gross Clinic (Figure 22)*. Another reflection of the painting's mood can be discovered in the face and attitude of Eakins himself. He was painted by his wife at the right, attentive, listening to an explanation he probably did not require.

Dr. Agnew was made famous in his own time by his attendance upon President Garfield, who had been shot by a madman, and famous for a longer

42. DR. AGNEW (STUDY)
1889. 50⅜ x 32. Yale University Art Gallery, bequest of Stephen C. Clark.

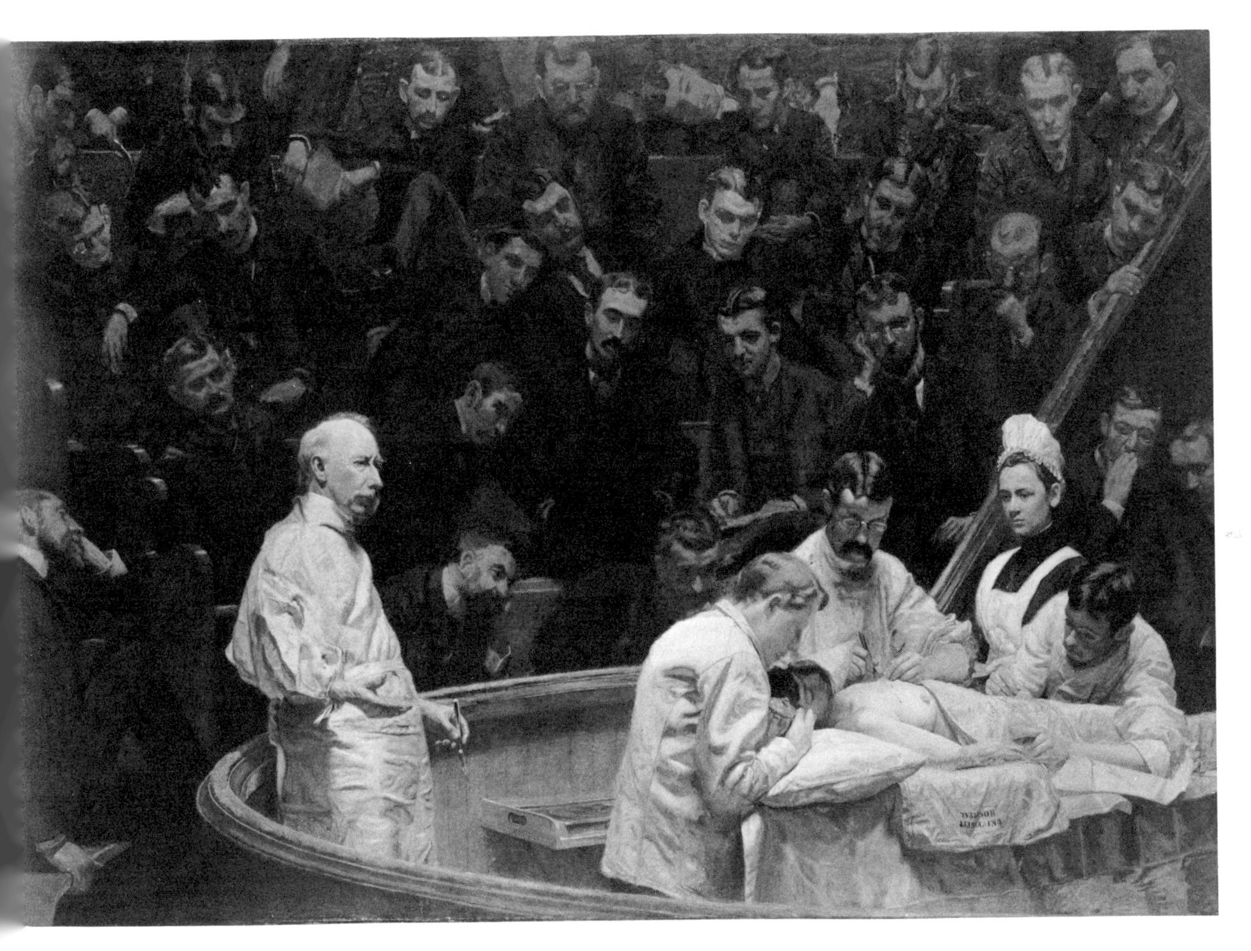

43. THE AGNEW CLINIC

1889. 74½ x 130½. University of Pennsylvania.

period by the recalcitrant idealist-as-artist who differed with him over certain matters of convention. In his lecture on "The Relation of Social Life to Surgical Disease" Dr. Agnew had, in an inspired passage, enumerated the damages done to the female anatomy by the Victorian corset. At another time he was to provide an illustration of his conviction, expressed in that lecture, that convention was far more powerful than science in the ordinary affairs of men. When Eakins painted blood on the doctor's hands, he ordered it removed. He was unshaken by the artist's plea for truth to nature. There is some blood in the painting, but there is no blood on Dr. Agnew's hands.

The Agnew Clinic was well received by the students who had commissioned it but not by Philadelphia's directors of taste to whom Eakins was more than ever demonstrably a butcher. They refused to hang *The Agnew Clinic* in the Academy's 1891 Exhibition, and so they revealed once more their aesthetic, intellectual and moral bankruptcy, the pathetic failures of a class pretending to aristocracy. For plainly what Eakins had taken as sacred had in fact been rendered with something like divine passion.

However indignant and sure of himself, however much he was supported by artists and critics who knew better, Eakins was deeply injured by this repetition of the response to *The Gross Clinic*. Neither the city nor a class were alone, it should be said, in failing to understand the painting. The dark force of the genteel was widespread in the land, when, in the spring of 1892, the Society of American Artists rejected *The Agnew Clinic* for exhibition. Eakins was prompted to tell the Society where he stood:

> I desire to sever all connections with the Society of American Artists . . . For the last three years my paintings have been rejected by you, one of them the Agnew portrait, a composition more important than any I have ever seen on your walls.
>
> Rejection for three years eliminates all elements of chance, and while in my opinion there are qualities in my work which entitle it to rank with the best in your Society, your Society's opinion must be that it ranks below much that I consider frivolous and superficial. These opinions are irreconcilable. [Quoted by Goodrich, *Thomas Eakins, His Life and Work*, pp. 130-131.]

Meaningful images of community can probably only be generated by communities worthy of them, and Eakins felt himself forced to discover his meanings and his affirmations where he had always sought them to some degree, in isolated human figures. But that direction was hardly the only one his work and his inclination might have dictated.

DRAWN to define as nearly as he could the individuality of each of the students who posed for the audience in *The Agnew Clinic*, Eakins had revealed something like the Whitmanesque feeling for democracy, that romantic sense of the importance of the individual in the mass akin to Whitman's "personalism," here tempered by Eakins' sobriety and by the significance of the occasion. Romantic effects were more directly expressed in a number of head and busts of men painted in 1889 and 1890. In a portrait painted in 1884 of George Reynolds called *The Veteran (Figure 44)* mood had been as important as characterization. And mood had illuminated character, though without the kind of psychic penetration that marked the portrait of another bearded figure, Walt Whitman *(Figure 41)*, three years later.

Though the Whitman remained almost *sui generis*, there are strong echoes of it in a portrait of Franklin Schenck painted about 1890. Eakins responded to the poetic, unworldly qualities of Schenck's temperament and attempted to penetrate the picturesque appearance. The long hair and untamed beard of the art student were possibly a difficulty. In *The Bohemian (Figure 45)* light falls on the left side of Schenck's face, the head and bust tilted slightly to the right. The heavy use of shadow is more than a dramatic device. It lends depths to the dream of the contemplative man and Eakins views him with considerable sympathy. Yet the dreamer is at a remove from the anguished man, a type closer to the center of his interest.

Samuel Murray *(Figure 46)* was younger than either Reynolds or Schenck and he was also clean-shaven so that the romantic effect of his portrait (1889) is now more directly grounded in a reading of character through physiognomy. Weakness contends with strength in that face, and sensitivity and self-indulgence are set side by side, in the solid form of the portrait itself, in the sensual lips and dreaming eyes, in the line of the jaw, in the simplicity of the plain blue jacket and the mild affectation of the loose purplish tie. The promise of youth is undercut in a way by a softness, a lack of deeply defined intellectuality in the boy who was to become the closest companion of Eakins' later years. The immediate light in which we see Murray is the romantic one, as if his youthful, physical handsomeness had some timeless and typical quality apart from mortality. But the profound qualification of the romantic effect distinguishes the portrait and accounts for its life.

No such qualification seemed necessary when he painted, in 1890, Talcott Williams *(Figure 47)*, the learned editor of the *Press* who had introduced him to Whitman, and the portrait is entirely unequivocal in its implied admiration for the man. Its bold yet understated assertion of human signifi-

44. THE VETERAN

1884. 22¼ x 15. Yale University Art Gallery, bequest of Stephen C. Clark.

45. THE BOHEMIAN
About 1890. 24 x 20. Collection of the Philadelphia Museum of Art.

46. SAMUEL MURRAY
1889. 24 x 20. Mr. and Mrs. John Russell Mitchell.

47. TALCOTT WILLIAMS
1890. 24½ x 20½. Mrs. L. H. Seelye.

cance is an effect, in part, of the light striking the right side of his face and forehead. It is also a reflection of the painter's success in defining the special kind of individuality we observe in these romantic portraits. What we have, very interestingly, at this point in Eakins', in his sitter's and in his country's history, are portraits of an inwardness unconnected with any immediately personal sense of tragic recognition. In the portrait of Talcott Williams a vital intelligence significantly apprehends reality more in a mood of high seriousness than in anguish.

THE romantic effects expressed so directly — in paint, through a richness of tone and the sober drama of contrasting lights and darks, in the portraits themselves through their assertion of the high value of human consciousness — are exceptional to this period. These qualities go underground after this to lend a richness to more realistic studies. Something of what happened, in the movement toward the kind of vision that had always been latent in his work, could probably have been discerned in the three-quarter-length figure of Professor Barker painted in 1886, during the time of Eakins' difficulty at the Academy and a year before he met Whitman, where Eakins saw a very individual kind of understanding in tension with, but very much contained by, larger forces of character. Unhappily, this portrait was later cut down to head and bust size *(Figure 48)*. Eakins thought it one of his best. Barker had confronted the observer directly. The strength in head, body, arms and hands was animated by the inexplicable communication of an intelligence at work beneath the conventional appearance, an intelligence that has a breadth and a depth beyond anything one might have expected.

In three large full-length portraits of men his art and his reading of character advanced together, not surpassing the unassuming austerity of the Barker, but moving beyond it in their design, or in the depth or the complexity of their human discoveries. *Dr. Horatio C. Wood* (1899) *(Figure 49)* was a triumph of sheer style (reminiscent of an early Renoir), capturing an almost palpable mood of quiet sobriety apart from any easily discernible romantic intensity or psychological insight. Dr. Wood is thoughtful and learned and unpretentious as he sits behind his desk, holding a pen to his mouth. In his easy posture Eakins discovers the expansive personality quietly allied to the meditative and reflective one and the painting recalls, in this way, the very different portrait of Professor Rand *(Figure 10)* some fifteen years earlier.

Professor Fetter (*Figure 50*), painted in 1890, firmly establishes the ground

48. PROFESSOR GEORGE F. BARKER
1886. Original state. 60 x 40. Present owner unknown.

49. DR. HORATIO C. WOOD
1889. 64 x 50. Courtesy of The Detroit Institute of Arts.

50. PROFESSOR GEORGE W. FETTER
1890. 78 x 52. Philadelphia High School for Girls.

for the consistently intensive approach to character and personality characteristic of Eakins' later style. Composed of the most ordinary materials — the professor seated in his swivel chair, the open rolltop desk behind him, the worn oriental rug, the Bible beneath his left hand — the portrait produces effects inexplicable in terms of literal content alone. It may appear no more than a classic confrontation of the schoolmaster in his office, of the contented stability of a fat authoritarian old German, but there is a tension in it inexplicable in those terms. Alone in his office, isolated in that space, Professor Fetter is yet thrust out upon us, demanding our attention. There is a restrained energy in his quiet, brooding concern as he sits there cross-legged looking out, and a sadness beyond discipline in his eyes. The portly man has, surprisingly, a sensitive mouth and hands, and there is a curious illusion of youthfulness in him. These meanings flow beneath what is more directly rendered, and what for that matter strikes us first, the older man's reflection upon age and time, his absorption in memory. Injury and stoic powerlessness, a judgment of the world and a scrutiny of self are all implied by the professor's stare.

These profoundly rendered complexities of personality take, if it is possible, the *Portrait of a Lady (Figure 39)* one step further. To look back at the portrait of Dr. Brinton *(Figure 24)*, the only earlier seated full-length isolated figure of a man to achieve something like this kind of intensity, is to begin to understand how the mind of the painter has developed. The appeal of the *Brinton*, however much it embraced the contrary possibilities of existence, was single, direct. The effect of the *Fetter* is far more complex. Having grown immensely in his understanding of existence, Eakins communicates that understanding ever more powerfully.

To see the portrait of Professor George W. Fetter in the original requires a pilgrimage through a landscape that did not exist in 1890. I remind myself of this not in anger but in the effort to recover the past which nurtured the seeds of this wasteland. The landscape in 1890, seen from the trolley line that ran out into the countryside, was still pastoral and defenseless. Then the spirit of avarice behind the mean attempts to control public transportation in Philadelphia became the spirit that dominated the landscape of Broad Street. Now, north along that wide avenue lies the litter, the holy garbage of free enterprise, a drab decay awaiting resurrection, a rise in land values, the bulldozer, and new swarms of powerful ant men whose values will not be those of Professor Fetter. The Normal School has moved twice since Eakins' time, once to a new building in the same neighborhood a few blocks from Eakins' home on Mt. Vernon Street, and then again to avoid the dangers and the squalors of a changing neighborhood. It fled its dark Apollo and was transformed to the Philadelphia High School for Girls. No laurels grew among the rows of houses across from the school.

Professor Fetter is come at after a march past metal lockers. A painted plaster statue of Lincoln stands in the hallway. At the end of it, against a pink marble wall, the old man sits. The encounter gives meaning not only to the landscape of this quest, but to the sound of the school orchestra groaning in labor in the auditorium. In the retiring principal of a girls' school Eakins discovered a vigor, a feeling for life, a belief that went beyond knowledge and that distinguished the man.

In *Professor Henry A. Rowland (Figure 51)*, done in 1891, Eakins examines a scientist not a humanist, a man in whom one may detect an emotional limitation, as if the painter were in part concerned to observe the consequences of work limiting the growth of understanding or the development of a more humane knowledge. Professor Rowland has the stare not merely of the posed sitter but of the scientist caught in abstraction, a lean cerebral man caught up in a dream of numbers. In his posture one reads a devotion to science and a rectitude that are both exemplary, and, one prays, not mere historical curiosities. Professor Rowland's work was done apart from committees and corporations; the diffraction grating he holds in his hand was born from the forehead of Zeus after purely disinterested labor. Behind him, his assistant, the serious craftsman technician, is a less cerebral, less intellectually intense presence. Yet though Mr. Schneider may be more fully in contact with human realities than Rowland, his presence more nearly defines than limits the observer's sense of Rowland's humanity. Eakins had a profound sympathy for the man. The painting achieves a warmth and depth quite apart from its apparent subject matter, drawing these in part from the human oppositions embodied in Rowland, caught up in his abstracted mood as he sits there, and his assistant, standing in the shadows of the laboratory, another of Eakins' silent choric figures. [*See note, page 289.*]

In the decade preceding his study of Mrs. Letitia Bacon (1888) the only important completed portrait as such of a woman alone had been that of his wife. One other, of Mrs. William Shaw Ward (1884), had not been finished. The portrait, painted in 1878, of Mrs. John H. Brinton *(Figure 52)* had been the last of the series which included the portraits of Margaret

51. PROFESSOR HENRY A. ROWLAND

1891. 80 x 54. Addison Gallery of American Art, Phillips Academy, Andover, Mass.

52. MRS. JOHN H. BRINTON
1878. 24½ x 20⅛. Mr. and Mrs. R. Meyer de Schauensee.

(Figure 7), Katherine *(Figure 8)* and Elizabeth *(Figure 9)*, works that discovered beauty through character and mood as well as through design originating in psychologically expressive gesture. In the study of Mrs. Brinton there was beauty in the head looking diagonally down past the left hand to a red fan, in the introspective force of the averted eyes, in the forearm, wrist and hand, in the subdued yet rich coloring. Yet there was no flattery in this work, and no idealization. For the most part the women who sat for Eakins could find neither beauty nor reassurance in his portraits of them. He had to learn to disregard their responses when he began to paint their portraits again.

There is a simple strength of form in the three-quarter-length portrait of Letitia Bacon *(Figure 53)* whose upright carriage, emphasized by the strong vertical line of her shawl, lends power to the subtle force of the tilted head, looking downward and out. The rich tones of this work might have lent distinction to a more conventional and fashionable portrait but again Eakins makes no concession to any generalized idea of beauty. Mrs. Bacon's eyes are open and staring, and she shows, in that posture, the beginnings of a double chin.

The meditative mood implies quiet, minor recognitions, a reflection upon expectancies or the lack of them as well as upon the past. The world of Mrs. Brinton had been altogether less problematical. Accustomed to Eakins' vision we may not immediately realize that this is an unusual view of a woman in an evening dress, this discovery of elegance and of grandeur in the moment of self-examination that has begun to turn subtly outward. [*See note, page 289.*]

The portrait of Miss Amelia Van Buren (about 1891) *(Figure 54)* sharpens its statement of character yet remains as richly suggestive in achieving its effect, as forcefully elusive, and more adventurous in color and design. Miss Van Buren has drawn herself to one side of the chair that Katherine and Mrs. Brinton had sat in; she looks into the strong light falling upon her face and upon her pink-and-white flowered dress. Alert and sensitive, she examines the world with an intelligence and a quiet sort of knowing if not a cynicism. In the sensitive mouth, the face narrowing down rapidly from the widely spaced cheekbones, the strong right hand holding the fan, the more delicate hand supporting her head, Eakins saw a personality in tension with its world, and perhaps subdued by the character it had earned there. Miss Van Buren is graying, disappointed, her dress an elaborate and beautiful statement of unfulfillment. She is a small woman with a large

53. MRS. LETITIA WILSON JORDAN BACON
1888. 59 x 39½. The Brooklyn Museum.

54. MISS AMELIA VAN BUREN
About 1891. 45 x 32. The Phillips Collection, Washington.

55. HOME RANCH
1890. 24 x 20. Collection of the Philadelphia Museum of Art.

56. GIRL IN A BIG HAT
1888. 24 x 20. Joseph H. Hirshhorn Collection.

57. THE RED SHAWL
1890. 24 x 20. Collection of the Philadelphia Museum of Art.

brooding spirit, almost masculine in the quality of her understanding. Caught in this still moment she is extraordinarily and intensely alive. Design is too poor a word for what Eakins discovers to give movement and vitality to his vision. Degas never achieved more. In its discoveries and restraints *Miss Van Buren* is a great triumph, one in which the aesthetic force of color and design is hardly distinguishable from psychological and moral insight.

When one accepts the narrow range within which Eakins came increasingly to work, the varieties of possible impressions within that range as well as the occasional breaks from it — the *Cowboys in the Bad Lands, Home Ranch (Figure 55)* and the other cowboy paintings of this period, as well as *The Agnew Clinic (Figure 43)* itself — continue to surprise and to reassure us of the unfailing flow of his deep human vitality. [*See note, page 289.*] Among other portraits of women, two which fall between that of Letitia Bacon *(Figure 53)* and Amelia Van Buren *(Figure 54)* strike very different notes. That of Lillian Hammett, *Girl in a Big Hat* (1888) *(Figure 56)*, is remarkable for what it achieves through simplicity of design and the most restrained palette, a strikingly beautiful portrait of a plain, bespectacled young woman. It recalls, in its way, that extraordinary first portrait of his sister Frances *(Figure 3)*, beautiful not simply because of its honesty, but because the rich, embracing (one is tempted to say compassionate) consciousness of the painter conceived its design as a perfect complement to his vision which could reveal beauty where the conventional mind must have seen merely the homely or the ugly. Then in 1890 in *The Red Shawl (Figure 57)*, he found another subject apart from the canons of "high art" in Philadelphia, in the youth, beauty and sensitivity of a young mulatto woman. Her large-eyed stare takes in an entire world of sadness within the American experience, one almost untouched by other American artists in Eakins' time. [*See note, page 290.*]

The end of this four-year period of creativity culminates, in 1892, in another sort of image, the isolated performer, a standing woman singing, and no painting was to more fully reveal the purely responsive, naïve and noble quality of his subjective nature than *The Concert Singer (Figure 58)*. In Weda Cook's youth, vitality and beauty, in all her unselfconscious and unassuming physicality, and in the communicated force of life flowing through her he expressed an idealism grounded in the most profound sense of physical reality.

58. THE CONCERT SINGER
1892. 75 x 54. Collection of the Philadelphia Museum of Art.

A more sophisticated artist in some ways, Sargent could paint his portrait of Madame X in a way that any cultivated European could understand: he would know in what way the woman was beautiful, in what way she thought herself beautiful, and he could define precisely the social role she would play in a man's world. *The Concert Singer* explains none of these things. It is utterly without irony, accepting the performer and the performance at face value, and more, giving the girl's moment a monumental force and a significance that a European, even a Degas, might have considered disproportionate.

Weda Cook, a friend of both Eakins and Walt Whitman (she had set "O Captain, My Captain!" to music), posed for this life-size full-length work over a period of two years, starting each session by singing "O Rest in the Lord" from Mendelssohn's *Elijah* so that the painter could observe the action of her throat and facial muscles. The time he took for this very American masterpiece may hint of renewed psychic difficulty, but the work itself is the most unequivocal affirmation of life and of art. It stands as a monument before a period of disruption and uncertainty, before Eakins could finally fix upon the themes of mortality, of isolation and of moral and psychic recognition as the only meanings he cared deeply to explore in his portraiture, the only ones which might give release to his repressed vitality.

WHEN Dr. D. Hayes Agnew died early in the spring of 1892, Eakins and his pupil Samuel Murray took plaster casts of his head, face, and hands. Not long afterwards they crossed the Delaware to Camden to take Whitman's death mask, and casts of his hands, and chest. Whitman's head appears small in death, the nose prominent, the cheeks sunken. His chest is thin, wasted. Beneath his beard the poet hid a receding jaw. Eakins and Murray signed the bust at its base, and the date, May 6, 1892. [*See note, page 290.*]

10

I stood day after day while he patiently transcribed me — for his method stuck closely to the object; and I watched his large underlip, red and hanging; his rather lack-luster eyes, with listless lids; his overalls of blue . . . and his woolen undershirt, the only upper garment.

He was very silent.

(They visit Eakins' sister at her farm:)

He ate eagerly, in shirt-sleeves, with little attention to the children at the table, talking hardly at all.

(Morris's horse falls:)

Eakins paused and looked back with a rather listless attention.

— Harrison Morris, *Confessions in Art*

I taught in the Academy from the opening of the schools until I was turned out, a period much longer than I should have permitted myself to remain there.

My honors are misunderstanding, persecution and neglect, enhanced because unsought.

— Eakins, Letter to Harrison Morris, April 23, 1894

FOR the better part of six years following the death of Whitman, Eakins appears to have painted only fitfully. In 1893 the only recorded portrait is of Dr. Da Costa *(Figure 59)*. The next important portrait, of Frank Hamilton Cushing *(Figure 60)*, was not painted until late 1894 or 1895. He was at work again in 1895 and part of 1896 when he completed substantial portraits of Riter Fitzgerald *(Figure 61)*, of John McClure Hamilton *(Figure 62)* and of Rudolph Hennig, *The Cello Player (Figure 63)*, but the illness of his niece, Ella Crowell, in 1896 and her suicide in 1897 had a profound effect upon him, and he painted little in either year. By the middle of the decade, the Art Students League having disbanded, Eakins had entirely given up his itinerant teaching in New York, in Philadelphia, and in Washington. He had tried to teach at Drexel Institute in Philadelphia and had been forced to resign after insisting once more upon the absolute nude in his life class. "I have never discovered that the nude could be studied in any way except the way I have adopted. All the muscles must be pointed out. To do this all the drapery must be removed," he told Riter Fitzgerald. The sanity of Fitzgerald, who defended him in the *Philadelphia Item*, was of no help; his deep sense of personal injury and his profound frustrations had made painting almost impossible. [*See note, page 290.*]

His personal bitterness did not carry over directly into the portraits of this time, but it found expression in the development of their meditative quality, in the continued deepening of psychological analysis, and in a renewed discovery of the tragic. An uncertainty not of vision but of the will marks much of the work he could not finish, as if he felt he could not say what he had come to know, or as if the forms of his vision had become disturbing even to himself. There is of course a simpler answer for his failure to complete a portrait: If a sitter did not like what he saw, he might not return, and Eakins was unlikely to conclude his work without the model before him.

Dr. Jacob M. Da Costa, whom Eakins first painted in 1892, must have objected to his portrait *(Figure 59)* in terms Eakins could accept, however despairingly, for he destroyed it and painted another in 1893. It hangs in a hallway of the Pennsylvania Hospital today, down a corridor from Benjamin West's *Christ Healing the Sick.* Dr. Da Costa is seated in a straight chair, legs apart, hands on his thighs, erect, though not stiffly so. Tension does not distinguish the man; his posture suggests a calm, but one that has followed upon some deep and pervasive fatigue. His eyes convey the same sort of weariness. The mouth is unsmiling, firm, almost pursed, yet the flesh sags. But the droop of the shoulders, the sag of the body and the weariness in the face are confronted, restrained, and ordered at last by a quality of character written in every line of this work. Seated there in his dull black, Dr. Da Costa is a study of worn strength, a man whose understanding extends for this moment beyond the flesh.

The doctor was still not pleased, beset as he was by other images of himself. Did the noted diagnostician want a work that would attest to his eminence in his profession — possibly something more on the order of Eakins' portrait of his associate, Dr. Agnew? Eakins saw the mortal isolated man and he thought enough of him to paint a great and honest portrait, a coherent and moving response to an entire life. Dr. Da Costa did not find it enough.

The other portraits in the corridors of the hospital exhibit the common failings of that art and also serve, it may be, as reflections of the aesthetic sensi-

59. DR. JACOB M. DA COSTA
1893. 42 x 34. Pennsylvania Hospital.

bilities of the medical men who commissioned them. In the attitudes or lack of attitudes struck (the consistent absence of arms, legs and hands in the portraits is a disturbance, though it is true that these features, executed with the same competence as those heads, shoulders, and vests, would add little to the sum of the world's beauty), in the smiling faces, in the complete absence of imagined form, in coloring which derives from the twin contemporary arts, that of the tinted photograph and of the undertaker trained in cosmetology, the artists and the men who commissioned them show themselves if not true Philadelphians, then Philadelphians who can acquiesce in the banal and the vulgar and find these qualities less disturbing than any achieved depth of human insight.

These are contemporary examples of the art. In a chamber of the Philadelphia College of Physicians there is another portrait of Dr. Da Costa painted in his own time that may have given the physician more satisfaction than the Eakins. It is larger, and in the frozen daguerreotype quality of the face there is a fatuousness and a banality that Dr. Da Costa could have found pleasing, for it is typical enough of the nineteenth-century view of rectitude; the sitter might be ugly if he were sufficiently frozen and dull. Dr. Da Costa is seated straight on, his head turned slightly, he has legs and hands, and he is planted in a large chair. It is a perfectly meaningless piece of work, a somewhat muddy document calculated not to offend a medical man.

FRANK HAMILTON CUSHING, his aesthetics and his young manhood formed in another culture, his vision unaffected by Philadelphia's genteel smog, was capable of appreciating what Eakins made of him. He had been twenty-three when his essay on Zuñi fetishes was published by the Bureau of Ethnology in 1880, thirty-seven when Eakins painted him in the costume of a Zuñi Priest of the Bow — a thin, wasted figure, his deeply pockmarked face that of a person twenty years older. Eakins frequently painted his sitters older than they were, as if age would show ever more clearly the fulfillment of character. It was the role of prophet, one Hawthorne might have appreciated (I am thinking of a story called "The Prophetic Pictures") and it usually disturbed his sitters. His view was not the social one, and the prophecy of fulfillment did not imply success in social terms. The portrait of Cushing *(Figure 60)* is a moving image of social failure and, in its way, a prophecy of death, for Cushing, his health broken by years of illness and hardship during his exploration of the Southwest was to die five years after Eakins painted him.

For the first time in the portrait of a man Eakins used the form he would explore in a number of later works, the life-size, full-length standing figure.

60. FRANK HAMILTON CUSHING
1894 or 1895. 90 x 60. Thomas Gilcrease Institute, Tulsa, Oklahoma.

Chase had painted Whistler that way. Whistler had been using the form, and Sargent, of course, but its meaning was to be radically different for Eakins. For Sargent the full length was often an opportunity for the exhibition of a dashing brushwork by which the social pretensions of his subject might most suitably be displayed. For Eakins the act of standing came to evoke the character and intelligence of the subject frequently in tension with some pervasive sense of the difficulties of plain mortality. In this he also differs from Velásquez whose full-length standing figures he had seen at the Prado. Velásquez is typically concerned with an unequivocal vision of human dignity, Eakins with the dignity of men who bear a deeper burden of personal consciousness.

Eakins submitted the Cushing to the Pennsylvania Academy exhibition of 1895-96 and it was rejected. The *Tanagra* of Mr. Anshutz, a large dull portrait of a bored woman, was acceptable to the directors of the Academy probably because it was empty of ideas. Was Eakins' large, warmly colored work too gaudy for their tastes, too much, in their judgment, like the colored posters of wild-west shows? Or did they detect an offensive idea in it?

Cushing, in Indian dress, standing in the center of a room in a Zuñi pueblo (reconstructed, for the portrait, in Eakins' studio), looks soberly down, holding in his magnificently rendered hands two ceremonial fetishes. But the painting does not indulge in the picturesque for its own sake, for it celebrates a disappearing culture and the dying man who devoted his life to studying it. Tragic possibility is written in Cushing's face, in an understanding that is beyond solace and in the emaciated figure of the man. He looks down, an anguish in his features, and a calm. It is a vision of the moral force of intellect inseparable from the tragic sense of life, and of an endurance that is both intellectual and physical, transcending both what is accidental to body and to individual experience. The man exists alone and in the broader experience of the age, expressing his reverence for a civilization being engulfed and destroyed in nineteenth-century America. Though Eakins was to discover other meanings in later powerful full-length portraits, none was to exceed this great masterpiece in conception or in effect.

A work in this form more nearly approaching the ideal of Velásquez is the portrait of John McClure Hamilton *(Figure 62)*, a sober figure but hardly a tragic one. Though Hamilton was an eminently successful portraitist in his time, Eakins chose to show him with none of the tools of his craft about. Isolated in this way and staring off to the right, Hamilton is observed in quiet self-contained reflection, neither in a mood of entire complacency, nor in one of agonized introspection. It is the stance of a man whose confidence is

61. RITER FITZGERALD
1895. 76 x 64. The Art Institute of Chicago, Friends of American Art Coll., Goodman Fund.

62. JOHN McCLURE HAMILTON
1895. 80 x 50¼. Wadsworth Atheneum, Hartford.

63. THE CELLO PLAYER

1896. 64 x 48. The Pennsylvania Academy of the Fine Arts.

grounded in a personal achievement that has been socially recognized. The body's weight and substance are less burdens than they are the physical instruments of his success. This portrait of the meditative man is perfectly unequivocal; there is no irony in it. [*See note, page 291.*]

If it is sometimes difficult to distinguish between this kind of grave meditative sensibility capable, one assumes, of comprehending the tragic, and the sense of tragic intensity itself, an occasional work has so pronounced an effect that its meaning is unmistakable. Among Eakins' portraits of painters none is so moving as that of Charles Linford *(Figure 64)*, a now forgotten landscapist in whose unfinished portrait, painted in 1895, the tragic effect is associated with the artist's vocation. Eakins uses identifying objects as only a great master can, not only as things in themselves, but as objects whose meanings enter the realms of human symbolism and psychological implication. Now Charles Linford holds his palette and brush and stares off at no visible landscape. This portrait, certainly not among his better known works, is one of Eakins' great surprises. No reproduction can suggest its power in evoking that guarded sense of tragic recognition characteristic of his most intense work.

There is a connection between Linford's rigid pose and the sense of self-discovery, of sudden apprehension or revelation. In the high dome of the nearly bald head held back and erect, in the grayish eyes staring to the right, there is the look again of a man facing death more than memory. It is his personal anguish we feel, that of a man caught in an understanding of his own mortal failure, his own futility.

Eakins' compassion never approaches sentimentality. In that quiet, luminous face he probes for the kind of intelligence and understanding he discovers there, a sensitivity, but not a great force, no more powerful than the figure is innately powerful. We are conscious of the man's thin legs and of his body, neither healthily spare nor vigorously weighty, and we have a sense, as in the Da Costa *(Figure 59)*, of the meaning of human fragility and weariness to the man himself. He holds himself erect in the face of recognition.

The few portraits of women painted in the mid-nineties represent, pictorially, no advance from the work that had preceded them. It is as if he had given over any attempt to find delight in the simplest variations of classical form that had claimed his attention only a few years before, in the meaning

64. CHARLES LINFORD
1895. Unfinished. 48 x 36. IBM Collection.

of a standing pose, of arms and hands, of a chair or of a patterned dress. Yet these portraits have their inestimable value for they are visions of women seen by our greatest portraitist when, very nearly on the dry bedrock of his creative energy, he could still respond to beauty where others might not have seen it, and ever more deeply to some kind of ultimate discovery of existence by the women themselves. A quality of beauty, as he perceived it, had to move him, and then it is as if he meant to see whether that quality, whatever it was, would stand up under the most austere treatment, in which any accessory other than dress itself would have appeared the merest vanity. He chose evening dress frequently because he thought it beautiful; as he used it, it tended to underline the distance between the hoped-for and the real world. In the portrait of Mrs. Cushing, done in 1894 or 1895, the ring of light formed by forehead, throat and arms and broken by her dark evening dress is the exact pictorial equivalent of the painting's mood of understated pathos, in the vision of a young woman soberly lost in thought, yet still at some remove from any kind of tragic recognition *(Figure 65)*. This portrait is a lesson in the restraints and perceptions of Eakins' deeply responsive nature and it is especially difficult to find verbal equivalents for the artistry and the human tact expressing themselves so absolutely as they do here. Mrs. Cushing's arms and hands are heavy, her gut bulges, the musculature of throat and neck is revealed, and she is beautiful.

Maud Cook's *(Figure 66)* youthful beauty — Eakins painted her in 1895 — revealed in the light falling on the right side of her face and throat and upon her bust may appear, at first glance, more typical than individual, yet we recognize his hand in more than the uncommon emotional depth implied by the pensive attitude. It is there in the modeling of the lips, in the great full musing brown eyes, in the almost tactile softness of the skin. The hair, no ornament, is pulled back to reveal forehead and neck, and there is a certain heaviness in those features.

Though these portraits may appear superficially alike in their pensive moods and in the attitudes of their sitters, as each head is tilted, the subject looking down and away into some unseen distance of memory or dream, Eakins never developed a stock response to character. *Mrs. James Dodge* (1896) *(Figure 67)* tilts her head upward and the gesture stands for what the portrait as a whole communicates, the vitality, the human warmth and the openness to the world of a woman competent to deal with it. Eakins' brush moves with a freedom and a certainty in rendering the yellowish-green velvet evening dress, and in the background ranging from the browns of the left through the greens and dark greens of the right. Against it the clear-eyed woman radiates her strong confidence in life and an elegance inseparable from her vitality. [*See note, page 291.*]

That sort of response to life, it is true, became less frequent in his work, and what usually strikes us about these portraits is the mysterious beauty, beyond representational purpose, associated with varying degrees of sadness. In the unfinished portrait, about 1898, of Anna Lewis *(Figure 68)* for instance, the girl is not conventionally pretty as she sits there in her gray party dress looking off. Yet this painting has the haunting effect of beauty achieved through its grave simplicity of design and through the austere yet vital and sensual handling of its low-keyed palette. The girl appears to look through time, and the prophecy of emerging consciousness weighted by a sense of the world is written in those features and in that attitude.

IN the portraits of mature women Eakins is more troublingly unable to finish and so to fully clarify the implications of what he sees. Yet these works have their own startling power, the force of direct perceptions vigorously established before they break off. In the small portrait study of Miss Emily Sartain *(Figure 69)* the woman stands full length against the blocks of color, her right arm back, her open left hand at her side, a kind of aristocratic assertion in the stance. She is the professional whose womanliness has been eroded by her profession, but she is more. The imperious quality in that carriage and the force that shines out like some great light from that brilliantly finished head, from those penetrating eyes, the firm mouth, the high strong forehead, contrasts strangely with the yellow ball dress, the white-lace collar and bodice. It is a severe view of a woman whose disturbing masculinity can show itself in so aggressively feminine a pose. The repressions of the age are in this study; we are conscious of a violence in the effort of character to contain its frustrations. Whatever Emily Sartain thought of it, Eakins could not bring the study to completion in the large portrait it appears to promise. [*See note, page 292.*]

The pattern repeated itself in the unfinished portrait of Mrs. Samuel Murray *(Figure 70)*, whom Murray brought to sit for Eakins in 1897. Miss Jane Dean Kershaw was Murray's fiancée for some twenty years before he married her in 1916, and there is sexual repression, frustration, and something very like controlled hysteria in Eakins' view of her. She appears middle-aged but she was in her twenties when she sat for him. This thin intense woman stares wide-eyed at no corporeal object. Her large staring eyes, the tilt of her head and the cast of her firm mouth and jaw are set against her beautifully executed hands, the left open in her lap, the right twisted backward to rest

65. MRS. FRANK HAMILTON CUSHING
1894 or 1895. 26 x 22. Collection of the Philadelphia Museum of Art.

66. MAUD COOK
1895. 24 x 20. Yale University Art Gallery, bequest of Stephen C. Clark.

67. MRS. JAMES MAPES DODGE
1896. 24¼ x 20¼. Collection of the Philadelphia Museum of Art.

68. ANNA LEWIS
About 1898. 33 x 27¾. Joseph H. Hirshhorn Collection.

69. MISS EMILY SARTAIN (STUDY)
1890's. 23½ x 17½. Rita and Daniel Fraad Collection.

70. MISS JANE DEAN KERSHAW (MRS. SAMUEL MURRAY)
1897. 40 x 30. University of Nebraska, Frank M. Hall Collection.

on her hip. The artist had recorded gesture, discovered design and probed so deeply, one feels, that once again he could complete neither the three-quarter-length portrait nor the head and bust. Miss Kershaw looks out but avoids direct confrontation with the viewer. Beyond the "wistful almost distraught feminine spirit" that James Breckenridge saw in her is a sensitivity that has begun to move beyond disillusion, hardening into a resistance. It is a remarkable vision.

At the end of that decade of uncertainty with its signs of frustration and incompletion and its moving apprehensions of the tragic, Eakins emerged to produce the grand series of boxing paintings which derive from the epic sense of life always fundamental to his nature. These powerful affirmations of human endurance, achieved in the absence of bitterness and irony, are testimony to his strength and to his fundamental health. Yet they are not without their sadder meanings. In them the consciousness of time becomes atmosphere and setting for the classical and epic sense of body, and carnival is celebrated in full awareness of mortality.

The static effect of *Taking the Count (Figure 71)*, painted in 1898, derives, as it did in his earlier work, from a response to history as well as to biological time. Here, vision coerces the epic moment to a monumental stillness before life bursts loose again. The old criticism that Eakins cannot paint movement is not entirely relevant in this painting and elsewhere where the achieved effect is of so high an order. The posed and poised figures have been brought to a stop, and the elemental meaning each represents is defined in that mood of quiet yet forceful tension that flows beneath so much of his work. In balance with the latent power of the standing boxer is the meaningful vitality of the boxer taking the count and about to stand. Are they compositionally unrelated in any other way? Eakins seems concerned to define each of their attitudes in isolation, as if the stance itself were most important, and not its relation to some other posture. The relation is to something wider. The solid painting, the integrity with which each figure is rendered in this scene, the two boxers, the referee, the two attendants behind the ropes (one holding the lower rope of the ring, watching, the other counting, pointing), all contribute to an effect given a subtle resonance by the treatment of theme. The posters hung up on the gallery, simple documentary elements of the scene, colorful reminders of the late nineties, are parodies of the painting's meaning, light-hearted commentaries upon its serious purpose. The audience watching this encounter will be seen at other dramas, to see Louis Mann (the dandy in comic pose) as Hans Mix in *The Ballet Girl*, and Miss Clara Lip-

71. TAKING THE COUNT

1898. 96 x 84. Yale University Art Gallery, Whitney Collection of Sporting Art, given by Francis P. Garvan.

man in the *Telephone Girl* at the Walnut Theatre. It all coheres. History and time are suspended in this frieze, and the referee, caught in it, an isolated figure himself, is almost a sleepwalker during the count, an abstracted figure waiting.

In *Salutat* (1898) *(Figure 72)* the boxer leaving the arena raises his right hand in a salute to the applauding spectators. Unlike Bellows, who was to see boxing in another light entirely, through a vision like Goya's, the savagery of the fighters in terrific movement, the grotesque animal physiognomies of the spectators screaming encouragement, Eakins accepts the gladiatorial idea entirely without irony. There is a decorum in the excitement of these well-dressed Philadelphians, and a decorum as well as a realism in the procession of men leaving, one of the seconds with a towel, the other with his bucket, sponge and bottle. The painting has the effect of a pagan religious rite in this expressed reverence for the figure of the hero. . . . Curiously, in the light full on his body, his skin is almost pallid, a yellow white, a gray white, except for the face and neck, as if Eakins wished more to emphasize anatomy itself, and the weight of the standing figure.

The audience is thrust further into the background in *Between Rounds* (1899) *(Figure 73)*, a sea wash of humanity against whom the isolated boxer is seen. In the oil sketch for the painting the face of the boxer has the heavy insolence of youth, full of the pulsing blood of life. But in the finished painting he is a man with a fine, strong nose, thoughtful, abstracted as he waits for the timekeeper's signal.

Time asserts itself in the faces of older bearded men among the audience and the very atmosphere of the scene, the sense of smoke filling the arena, is the atmosphere of time. One's eye moves from the boxer to the spectators to the timekeeper, to the seconds. The timekeeper marks the suspended moment between rounds. One young handler in his blue shirt waves a towel. The other, bent over the boxer (the massive figure of Elwood McClosky, "The Old War Horse") holds a waterbottle by the neck in his powerfully drawn left hand. These are actors in a ritual whose elements of timelessness, monumentally conceived, are set once more against a chorus now marking time past. And the moment passes under the timekeeper's hand.

Taking the Count, *Salutat*, and *Between Rounds* in effect form a triptych celebrating human endurance through these images of the man downed, the victor, and the boxer waiting. There is no image of utter failure and defeat. Their epic effect is not in the grossly heroic or postured and not in the violently dramatic. It flows from the habitual restraints imposed upon vision and design, now exercised by the older craftsman to produce a solidity, a monumentality, an effect of permanence and unassuming grandeur still drawing its paradoxical vitality from assertions of mutability and mortality.

The boxing paintings throw our recollections back a quarter of a century to the great rowing scenes in which Eakins had expressed his feeling for personal, for biological and for historical time through the technique learned from Gérôme, the technique of the near view, of objects seen with an almost surreal clarity. Now the mature style of the master expresses itself through the technique of the distant view, more open, broad, bold, more appropriate to the profound detachment of the older man.

For Eakins, much of the 1890's was a period of creative impotence. In 1892 he had sculpted the horses for the equestrian figures of Lincoln and Grant on the Brooklyn Memorial Arch; in 1893, the bronze relief of the Battle of Trenton Monument. But, for the rest, he was offered few opportunities to find other directions for his creative powers. He had continued to suffer from significant public refusals to show his most important work, most notably in the Pennsylvania Academy's refusal to hang *The Agnew Clinic* in 1891, and in its rejection of the portrait of Frank Hamilton Cushing, in 1895. He had not recovered, and, indeed, never would fully recover, from the loss of his position at the Academy; the fading away of the Art Students League and the incident at Drexel Institute helped, in these years, to keep the wound open. His bitterness about his official treatment shows itself in the letter to Morris quoted at the opening of this chapter, and it is only a scrap of a letter, one of the few bits of personal biographical information that has come down to us from this time. In his private life, the insanity and suicide of Ella Crowell, for which his sister Frances and her husband held him in some way responsible, must have injured him profoundly. And lastly, unspoken in this history, is what must have been his and Susan Eakins' great disappointment in their failure to have children. He had been worn down by all these things. His range had narrowed inexorably, and the old power could show itself only in a portrait, or in an unfinished sketch. When we understand this, the resurgence of his force in the boxing paintings seems nothing less than miraculous. His feeling for body, so long repressed, had broken loose with the old austere masculine force. But sadly, in his own history, it freed itself here and in his paintings of wrestlers *(Figure 74)* only for this moment. When toward the end of his career he painted the nude again, it was by way of return to the old theme of William Rush.

72. SALUTAT
1898. 50 x 40. Addison Gallery of American Art, Phillips Academy, Andover, Mass.

73. BETWEEN ROUNDS
1899. 50¼ x 40. Collection of the Philadelphia Museum of Art.

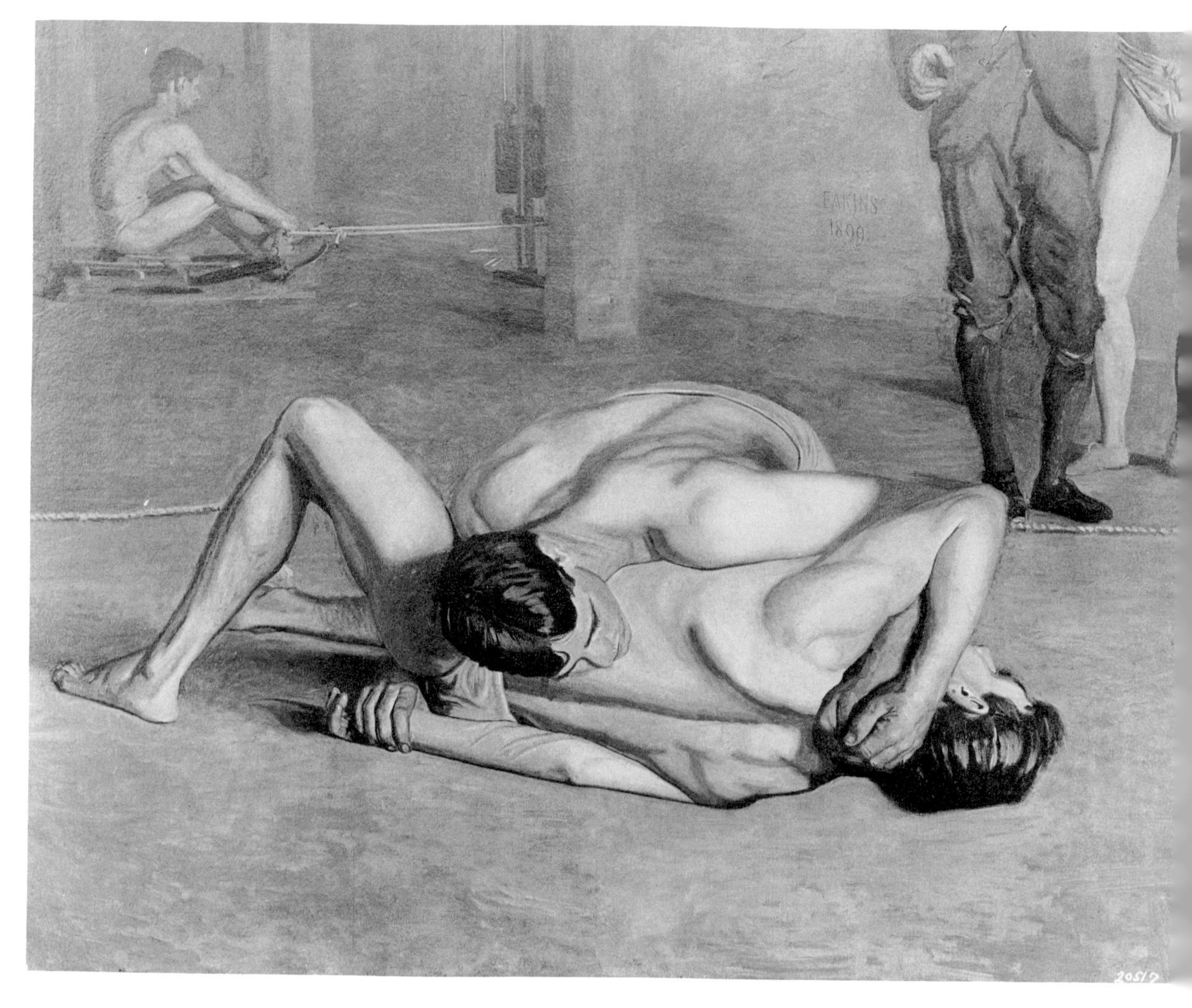

74. WRESTLERS
1899. 48 x 60. National Academy of Design.

11

> I'd a thousand times rather have the little study by M. Vibert we saw at the watercolour exhibition. There's nothing much in it, if you like, you could take it in the palm of your hand, but you can see the man's clever through and through: that unwashed scarecrow of a missionary standing before the sleek prelate who is making his little dog do tricks, it's a perfect little poem of subtlety, and in fact goes really deep.
>
> — Marcel Proust, *The Guermantes Way*

IN 1900 a Philadelphia collector named Peter Schemm published a catalog of his collection of paintings, a thick red volume stamped in gold which can still be found in some of Philadelphia's used-book stores. If there is another monument to the man or to his collection knowledge of it is not general. We know what he looked like. He had a handlebar moustache and a bow tie. He is immortalized in the frontispiece of this volume, planted upon a bench before the upright piano in his gallery, a portly figure wearing a dull look of self-satisfaction.

His collection was that of a man with few uncertainties about existence who wished nevertheless to be reassured and elevated by art in his own way. Peter Schemm delighted in the anecdotal and in the picturesque, in reassuring landscapes, in the virtues exhibited by simple folk, and in the portraits of cows. His favorite picture, the sub-frontispiece to his collection, was Jules Breton's *The Communicant*. It is a sturdy peasant holding a long candle and beads, his black-banded hat under his blue-jacketed arm, a generalized portrait of religious virtue in baggy costume pants, a picturesque work of sweet sobriety. Peter Schemm preferred that his art should neither see nor feel too much. It might express a restrained sentimentality or a mindless archness, though the military passions were not excluded. Intellectual content in a painting was an embarrassment; anything which might disturb might not elevate.

His massed trophies were the happy plunder from the studios of Europe's most splendid academicians. Among the names which one may or may not recognize today are Bouguereau, Vibert, Meissonier, Rosa Bonheur, Schreyer, Blommers (whom Eakins painted) and Gérôme. Gérôme's vision fastens upon its exotic objects. Here a galloping lion hung in the air pursues deer in a barren landscape, there Egyptians are seen at prayer before a mosque. There is a photographic sharpness in the work of Vibert and in that of other members of the Academy. Pleasant appearance is unequivocally rendered.

Peter Schemm's collection was sold at auction in New York before the decade was out. Bouguereau's *The Gardener's Daughter* brought $3200. "This," the catalog informs us, "is the full-length life-size figure of a dark-haired young maiden, bare footed and bare armed, dressed in a low bodice over a white chemise and a deep mauve skirt over a blue petticoat. She holds a bunch of roses with both hands and inclines her head to enjoy the perfume from a white rose."

On the whole Peter Schemm preferred his maidens decently clothed; he bought Henners, but no Henner nudes. Nevertheless, hidden at the back of the auction catalog there is the surprise we should have expected, a work by Professor Wilhelm Käay, *Psyche and the Butterfly*, which is described by the catalog in a circumlocutory passage of some charm: "Seated on a grassy bank a maiden, holding in her right hand a bunch of flowers, which rests on a diaphanous mantle across her lap, is watching a butterfly which has just lighted on her left foot. The sunlight falls upon the picture from above and behind, touching the fair hair, the sloping shoulders, the right forearm, the right hip and knees and throwing the rest of the figure into luminous shadow." This nude brought only two hundred dollars. Had a new taste begun to assert itself, rejecting the lifeless, the sentimental and the banal nudes that had become popular in American collections, or were the bidders embarrassed to offer money for so much coy flesh?

The smiles of these maidens were reckoned less valuable than the more spectacular exercises of Schreyer whose *Retreat* sold for five thousand dollars ("An arab sheik mounted on a white horse and holding a banner in his right hand is urging his animal to a rapid pace over the rocky ground, looking backward as he goes. He is followed by a number of armed attendants, all of whom are galloping at full speed, and those nearest the sheik are anxiously watching behind them"), and whose *Reconnoitre* went to Martin Beck for seven thousand dollars. Henner's ideal head, "the head and shoulders of a girl with flowing hair and turquoise blue draperies," sold to Knoedler and Company for only $1750.

Peter Schemm had never been tempted to purchase an Eakins. What place might one have had among his collection of sweet maidens, simple-hearted monks, farmyards, kittens, puppies and cows, or among the heroic posturings of men in battle?

Was Peter Schemm's collection representative of the taste of Philadelphia's elect, of the tastemakers and potential patrons of the arts in Philadelphia? He had more life in him, and was more adventurous than they. The great Philadelphia collections, among them those of Peter A. B. Widener, of John G. Johnson, and later, of Albert Barnes, were formed by eccentrics and men of energy who were not at all of that class. Widener was the son of a trucker, himself a butcher, who carved the foundations of his wealth from meat sold to the Union army. He had great energy, made money in public transportation, and built a more substantial collection than Peter Schemm's. He had the best academic advice and bought objects of unquestionable value with substantial pedigrees. Johnson, the son of a blacksmith, became the country's first great corporation lawyer. His collection was the expression of a strong inquiring intellect and of a developing aesthetic taste that fastened upon what it could find of the less expensive masterpieces of the Dutch, Flemish and Italian traditions. He also collected Corot, Constable and Degas. Barnes, that unlovable eccentric, had the right genealogy, but no money at first. He began to make it on Argyrol as Eakins began to tire, and although he bought the portrait of Dr. Agnew for something under five thousand dollars, he thought Eakins a mere academic. [*See note, page 293.*] He collected Renoir and was angered when Philadelphia thought his collection an abomination. He built a fortress in Merion to house it, excluded the Elite who now wished to see his pictures, and insulted them when he could. True art was for the initiates, for the students of the Barnes method alone. . . . Among these men only Barnes was interested in American art.

Philadelphians of family were not much interested in anything, except to hold on to what they had. When what they had began to decay and fall apart about them, increasingly west along Spruce Street, and then around Rittenhouse Square and Delancey Street, they moved out to a more verdant world accessible to the Pennsylvania Railroad. Whether it was Henry James or a bishop who in addressing them said, "I take it you are all members of the middle class," the remark was founded on the plainest truth. They believed in security, solidity and comfort; they frowned upon energy and intellect; it was not their intention, but they distinguished themselves, at last, by the absurdity of their pretensions to culture and to piety and by their belief in the inviolability of their dull families and their moribund traditions.

How was it possible for the young Eakins to expect patronage from this class, one as classically unsuited to be patrons of meaningful art as any in the history of modern Western civilization? Its blatant religious and aesthetic deficiencies were both characterized by a deep-seated failure of imagination, by the near systematic refusal to look profoundly at life. One collected, perhaps, family portraits in the English manner, for the same reason one joined the Episcopalian church, to establish one's credentials. Perhaps Eakins was misled by their dullness, taking it for a more intelligent sobriety; perhaps he saw in their attachment to family some sign of a larger virtue. No, that family-centered culture merely generated its own kind of genteel irresponsibility.

It was as communally destructive as it was socially regarding. Political responsibility extended no further than the interests of one's class; and a concern for the land was bounded by the perimeters of one's estate. Its concern was all for appearance; it was bound to fear any art which probed too deeply. Vision and intelligence made it uneasy. Religion became an adjunct of social pretension; there being no religious painting, painting had in some way to glorify that pretension. Any art, any personal vision which faced it on its own materialistic ground discovering intellectual or spiritual significance there was bound to appear vulgar or threatening. And as to Peter Schemm, one could only look upon his kind with condescension. Those people were very perfect in their dullness, and Peter Schemm's infantile light, his happy Veblenian acquisitiveness, the epigone of passion, might have shone brightly among them. [*See note, page 293.*]

We see our land, America, her literature, aesthetics, etc., as, substantially, the portrayal of our own physiognomy . . . and the deposit and record of the national mentality, character.

—Walt Whitman, *Democratic Vistas*

I am very grateful to you for getting me an important portrait to do, and not less for allowing me the use of your studio. . . .

If in your social visits you hear of portraits to be painted bespeak some for me on a business basis say twenty or twenty five per cent. Do you know I think an artist having a chance to see patrons could do no greater favor to them and to art itself than to show them how they can get their money's worth and not be cheated by the unscrupulous picture dealer.

—Eakins, writing to Frank Wilbert Stokes, a former pupil, in 1904

AFTER the beginning of the century Eakins began more actively to seek portrait commissions outside the circle of his friends, hoping, it may be, to compensate for the narrowing of his subject matter by widening his acquaintance with representatives of early twentieth-century civilization. His other motive in seeking commissions was to make money. He had always been sensitive about his father's support of him, and he had lived for the better part of his life dependent upon his father's money. Now the death of Benjamin Eakins reawakened the old hurt and the old necessity.

But he was no more equipped to find favor as a portraitist than he had ever been; he had never adjusted his art to social necessity and his sitters usually did not like what he saw in them. Some objected to his reasonable prices; others refused to accept his work, or accepted it and burned it. In the depths of his understanding he was an innocent who had hoped, like Inman before him, for a higher and purer taste, and their reactions embittered him.

He could be harsh, though he was less so than his "patrons" thought him.

In the most harsh of his portraits he was more inclined to view his sitters as victims than as agents. But the businessmen he painted were not comforted by the idea that they had failed in some important way. Furthermore, the late portraits cover an extraordinary range of human possibilities and never become, simply, uniformly sober studies of disappointed men and women. The perception of individual difference was the greatest flattery he could offer a sitter, and he continued to approach fairly well-defined possibilities of character with a radical openness always capable of achieving new subtleties of understanding and new intensities of insight.

The moments of recognition that he allowed his subjects, in which they appear simultaneously to grasp existence in its eternal aspects and a sense of their personal limitation, may appear to imply that his was ultimately a tragic vision. It was not, though it had always included tragic possibility. In certain portraits of men painted before 1900 (Cushing, Linford, his self-portrait; *Figures 60, 64, 84)*, and in others of women (Susan Eakins, *Figure 81)*, Adeline Williams *(Figures 82 and 83)*, something approaching tragic intensity was achieved when largeness of character was joined to some sudden or to some continuing apprehension of the darker aspects of life. Now, though the late work may evoke the tragic sense (Signora D'Arza, Mrs. Mahon, *Figures 111, 113)*, the underlying sense of human loss is frequently in tension with qualities of character that imply endurance (Leslie Miller, *Figure 93)* or with an understanding that includes some absolute sense of mortality (William Thomson, *Figure 90)*. The impression conveyed by the portraits as a whole is of a mind that continues to conceive of life in epic terms.

An Eakins portrait may carry with it a distinction which the work of no other American artist can match, and an intensity equalling or exceeding any to be found in the most penetrating portraits of the European masters. And while it would be vain to argue him the equal of Rembrandt or of Velásquez, he is not, in one's mind's eye, ill at ease in their presence. Working continually at cross-purposes with an audience that could understand neither his greatness nor his relation to the great tradition, he had to overcome more than the European masters to achieve anything at all. And when he breaks through, to penetrate appearance, to reveal meanings that are simultaneously personal and mirrors of some larger process, his vision moves us unexpectedly, profoundly, inimitably.

At the beginning of his last period are the remarkable portraits of his family completed in 1899 and 1900, before he began the active solicitation of portrait commissions. He painted his father in 1899, shortly before his death.

Although he was then eighty-one, and still the source of strength and emotional stability in that family, Benjamin Eakins *(Figure 75)* is caught in a questioning mood. It is not a senility we see in that head, but something like a profound speculative innocence in the face of larger knowledge, something curiously childlike in the quality of discovery underlying the meditative aspect. His recognitions, evoking their deep reflective sadness, are no things of the moment, for that most unassertive stoicism also written in those features, the restraint, the decorum and the order, had been exercised over a lifetime as a bulwark to understanding; yet he returns to the old truths as if they had been newly revealed.

The last portrait is more austere and more intensely emotional beneath its surface of restraint than *The Writing Master (Figure 76)* had been some seventeen years before. [*See note, page 293.*] *The Writing Master* was a classic example of the more profound possibilities of genre. It asserted something immutable and enduring in the monumental figure of the old man bent over his work, but it also saw Benjamin Eakins as an aging spirit of an old order whose devotion was to a passing craft. It counterpointed strength in the powerful head and in those sensitive yet formidable hands with the meticulous calligraphy itself, strength of character with the sense of frail mortality, the quality of endurance with the sense of change, achieving its effects with a richness of color and through the most unobtrusively challenging design.

Now Eakins tries to reveal as much about human endurance as a thing in itself, quite apart from craft or profession, in this vision of the isolated man. The theme of endurance in Eakins' late work, deeply connected with his feeling for his father, frequently engages the artist after the boxing paintings in the portraits of old men. That of his father, in its austere, mysterious and deeply moving way, opposes the idea of endurance with a meditation upon human destiny and the inevitability of loss. There is no questioning of the values that have supported life and neither hardness nor bitterness in the vision. The warm, mature response of *The Writing Master* has given way to an absolute confrontation of human existence.

THE portraits of William Macdowell *(Figures 77, 78, 79, 80)*, his father-in-law, dating from 1890 to 1904, show a bearded gray-haired man whose striking appearance might itself have been an obstacle to the revelation of character. In these craggy heads and busts, age, in some of its typical aspects, is Eakins' subject. He maps the deepening crater around an eye, the skin stretching tightly about the skull, the nose grown more formidable as the

75. BENJAMIN EAKINS
1899. 24 x 20. Collection of the Philadelphia Museum of Art.

76. THE WRITING MASTER: PORTRAIT OF THE ARTIST'S FATHER
1882. 30 x 34½. The Metropolitan Museum of Art, Kennedy Fund, 1917.

77. WILLIAM H. MACDOWELL, FATHER OF MRS. EAKINS
1890. 24 x 20. Yale University Art Gallery, Gift of Stephen C. Clark.

78. WILLIAM H. MACDOWELL
About 1891. 24 x 20. Walter G. Macdowell.

79. WILLIAM H. MACDOWELL WITH A HAT
About 1898. 28 x 21½. Walter G. Macdowell.

80. WILLIAM H. MACDOWELL
About 1904. 24 x 20. The Memorial Art Gallery of The University of Rochester, the Marion Stratton Gould Fund.

cheeks sink in shadow, the transiency of human appearance, the landscape of mortality. Yet the man emerges, upright and looking off, or his head bent and looking down, his arm resting on a chair, that marvelous old man's hand revealed, or looking out from beneath a large hat, less the prophet, less the lion, less ordered in dress, now merely an old body in a formless hat and overcoat. So that the last portrait is the more astonishing when he faces us directly, that fierce introspective stare implying the vision of some vast unattained moral order, violated by experience and by the *hypocrites lecteurs* who are not like him, who are neither brothers nor sons. The vision endures as life burns out and the old man asserts his difference. [*See note, page 293.*]

IN the brilliant, almost cruel (in the conventional sense) *Portrait of a Lady with a Setter Dog (Figure 39)*, Susan Eakins had seemed almost utterly overborne by her awareness, by the weight of her mortality, by the very world in which she and her husband lived. After a decade and a half, in 1899, Eakins returned to paint her again, isolated as he isolated his father from any visible contact with that world, in a work seemingly more objective, more harsh. And once more the emotional impact is, if it is possible to say so, far more concentrated than the effect of the earlier work. Susan Eakins *(Figure 81)* is seen in a strong light coming somewhat from the left, but falling full upon her face, against an almost black though luminous background, her head tilted slightly to the right, her eyes directly confronting the viewer, a large searching gray-eyed look. There is a clarity in it, a firmness and a strength that are again remarkably and utterly without bitterness. How the portrait includes yet turns away from that possibility is a mystery. Although Eakins raked his wife's face with the severest possible light to create an effect of tragic understanding that is almost entirely uncompromising, one comes away from the portrait with a feeling for something beyond the suffering and the loss imaged there, and it is impossible not to feel admiration for this woman so fully open to life, so fully aware. Susan Eakins was forty-seven when Eakins painted her; her dress, the open gray coat with the light on it, and the scarf held with a green-stoned pin, reveal the younger woman for whom hope existed in a still palpable past. It is Eakins' deep feeling for her that comes through at last, the recognition of qualities felt so intensely as to amount to a kind of romanticism.

AFTER the death of Benjamin Eakins, there came to live in the Eakins house Miss Mary Adeline Williams, then a woman of forty-five. Eakins had

81. MRS. THOMAS EAKINS
1899. 20 x 16. Joseph H. Hirshhorn Collection.

painted her mother in 1876, and the two families had long been friends. Miss Williams had been a close friend of Margaret Eakins, and Benjamin Eakins had asked her to come to stay at Mt. Vernon Street after Margaret's death in 1882. But she was twenty-seven then, his son had not yet married, and she did not come until Eakins and his wife asked her again, in 1900.

The two portraits of her are charged with opposed intellectual and emotional perceptions. In the austere 1899 portrait of *Addie, Woman in Black (Figure 82)*, there is injury and a muted stoicism in the introspective look and in the simple reading of anatomy, in the furrowed brow, the hard outlines of forehead, cheek and jaw, the strong nose, and the firm mouth. This woman endures by a quiet effort of will, half in shadow, half in light.

A year later he painted her again, turning her face directly into the light, deepening and modifying that first impression *(Figure 83)*. There is now a softness in the vision, as if he felt more certain that he could without injury strike through to the heart of Addie's womanliness. Her eyes are more fully open, and injury and disappointment are more directly written in them. Her head is less severely modeled; she wears a more colorful scarf and an elaborate striped blouse. But her eyes and mouth are most arresting, imaging an understanding of the failure precisely to achieve the fulfillment, to even approach the fulfillment implied by so much womanliness, so much human responsiveness . . . One of these portraits is in Chicago, the other in Philadelphia. But they are necessary to one another, and they should be seen together.

At fifty-seven Eakins painted himself *(Figure 84)*, much in the manner of Goya's self-portrait; he saw a heavy graying man, mortally and psychically weary. Is there bitterness in that vision? The steady exercise of character and the destruction of unrealized creative possibility had gone on for a lifetime, and the painter faces us with his stoical understanding of this meaning of his life. He reveals the man in the quiet judgment of the eyes, in the sagging flesh of his face, in the sparse untamed hair and beard. Yet what might have appeared the dramatic rhetoric of self-pity, this formidable and unblinking confrontation of human defeat, has the force of the most restrained, the most classic understatement.

In 1899 Eakins had painted his friend William Merritt Chase *(Figure 85)* whose experience as a painter in America had not been much like his own. The portrait of Chase succeeds without invoking the moment of discovery and without implying any malaise attributable to that age. It may almost be said to flatter, in its restrained way. There is human force and a monumentality in Chase's head, seen in left profile, head and bust leaning slightly backward diagonally from the left of the canvas, the slight disequilibrium creating a tension in that space. He is dressed impeccably in his gray suit; the white carnation in his buttonhole, the pince-nez with its gold clip on the black ribbon, the gold cravat pin and the precisely trimmed moustache and beard are marks of the successful artist secure in his social position, certain of his personal force. There is no trouble showing in that high forehead, no doubt in that eye.

Five years younger than Eakins, Chase died in the same year, 1916, full of honor. In 1899 he had been President of the Society of American Artists for ten years; he had been head of the schools of the Pennsylvania Academy for two, and was to continue in that role for ten more. Chase could not have lost his place at the Academy out of any obsessive necessity to bare the workings of the male pelvis to a mixed student group. His sense of propriety was absolute, and he coerced respect for his aesthetic views which were refinements of the taste of that era.

He was no provincial. In Philadelphia by way of Indiana, Munich and New York, he had all the urbanity of the Midwesterner who early decides to appropriate the culture of Europe and of the East Coast. Enlightened by travel, he returned to America ready to impale the occasional self-righteous Philistine whom he encountered upon the foil of his scorn; he had found the truth, and he had resolved to brook no difficulty with those who had not also discovered it. His intellectual limitations greatly aided his career. For Chase, truth lay in technique, and great painting in the treatment of surfaces. In his self-portrait (at the Detroit Institute of Arts), he was inspired to a certain controlled flamboyance. Behind the wild moustache is the theatrically conceived head of a man who believes in himself and in the aristocracy of talent.

The Sargent portrait of Chase at the Metropolitan is a comic work, the three-quarter-length portrait of a painter by a painter, both of them demonstrating the happiest sense of themselves — Sargent through the flash of paint, Chase by his pose, his brush in one highlighted hand, palette and brushes highlighted at the right, staring out full face, behind those great moustaches, with all the assurance of a grandee. Chase is all moustache and all posture, his face fierce and scowling in that light. Was he entirely happy with Sargent's product? "He has done me as a painter," he wrote, "and they say he has caught my animation — whatever that means."

From the beginning, following his return from Europe in 1878, Chase had

82. ADDIE, WOMAN IN BLACK (MISS MARY ADELINE WILLIAMS)
1899. 24 x 20. Courtesy of The Art Institute of Chicago,
Friends of American Art Collection.

83. ADDIE

1900. 24 x 18. Collection of the Philadelphia Museum of Art.

84. SELF-PORTRAIT
1902. 30 x 25. National Academy of Design.

85. WILLIAM MERRITT CHASE
1899. 24 x 20. Joseph H. Hirshhorn Collection.

been successful in advertising himself, in teaching, and in selling his work. He managed one-man shows for himself when these were rare. His studio was an atelier full of exotic things, not at all like the Eakins workshop. Students never objected to his methods. Summers, he taught them on Long Island where they helped to pay for his house; later he took them to Europe when the house at Shinnecock became too crowded with his eight children. His students paid for the Sargent portrait, destined for the Metropolitan. The master of surfaces had pleased them in capturing the outward look of their master.

The Eakins portrait is of a man by a man. In its restraint it speaks an honest respect for his friend, the most subtle reading of intelligence and of vitality. Chase was a fundamentally decent human being who by force of character and not by mere pose had managed, within the limits of his vision, to raise American standards and to give a new importance to the making of critical judgments.

Early in the century Walter Pach had seen Chase and Eakins together in conversation at an exhibition. "The personal verve and distinction of the brilliant technician," he recalled, "were arresting, even as his paintings were conspicuous in the exhibitions of his time. But the memory that comes back most vividly to me is that of the heavy figure of the older artist (older only by a few years, yet seeming of another generation) in whose slow impassive gestures there was something of the depth and dignity of his art."

Eakins' treatment of Chase was characteristic, in one way, of the difference between the portraits of his friends and of his "patrons." In general, he was kinder to friends than to the businessmen who paid or who objected to paying for his work. The strain of harshness in some of the commissioned work belongs to moral vision, not censure; equivalent effects in the portraits of friends and family were produced by his attempt to penetrate the anatomy of sadness. In the great portraits his imagination was intensely engaged; in the lesser ones head-and-bust likenesses reveal his craftsmanly skill, his intelligence and his tact, but they may suggest that the visual impression that prompted him to ask a sitter to pose had been deceptive. There are relatively few of these.

In either event, it may be difficult to tell through a reproduction whether or not he had achieved anything. Reproductions of a portrait apparently undistinguished by any inventiveness of design cannot suggest the subtleties of effect discoverable in the original where brushwork and paint itself may reveal meanings that have nothing to do with the representational intent.

His brush mysteriously discovers human ambiguity and antithetical possibility, simultaneously limning positive elements of character and the painter's sense of traits that are antilife. His sitters even in lesser works appear to participate in his understanding, and his brush unerringly records their participation. In the portrait of John Gest *(Figure 86)*, painted in 1905, the bearded old man stares off, his hands clasped in his lap, his body erect, the head slightly thrust forward. Eakins is gently responsive to the frailties, the timidities of age, but he sees a lingering harshness, even a tightness in the body so drawn into itself, as if the full comprehension of his mortality were suddenly being thrust upon his sitter. Gest's is hardly the meditative expression of Benjamin Eakins. If, in the treatment of the same theme, the portrait of his father was less complex and more powerful than this, no apology is required for the Gest. Pattern and character now move the artist in their own way. The beautifully painted curved wooden arms and back of Gest's chair are as much assertions of character as they are elements of design.

A LESS promising portrait is that of Charles E. Dana *(Figure 87)*, painted in 1902, whose image is usually preserved in the basement of the Pennsylvania Academy of Fine Arts. A reproduction may lead us to suspect that the judgment which keeps it there is entirely correct; there is nothing exciting in its composition and Eakins appears to have taken this handsome man at something like face value. The carefully trimmed moustaches, the cigarette holder in the right hand, the wedding ring on the left, the discreet rosette in the left lapel, the well-tailored dark coat carefully buttoned, the large white cravat, the high collar — these are necessary elements in any portrait of the perfect Philadelphia gentleman, and Dana was the very image of the type observed by Henry James at this point in history. Eakins painted the type, discreetly included the man's coat of arms, and yet managed to discover a man beneath the appearance. Close on, all the elements of dress, posture, gesture, and anatomy (the strong jaw, the fold of flesh beneath the chin, the large fleshy nose, the delicacy of the right hand, the heavily veined left) reveal a decaying ladies' man who, by an effort of character, can compose these features and keep as much of the flesh as firm as possible. It is in attesting to character asserting its formalized control over the processes of decay that Eakins gives credit to this carefully groomed gentleman. In the near hardness of his face and in his gray-blue eyes there is something that hints at its own understanding of decay, and of the significance of so much restrained personal style.

A more immediately impressive work is the portrait of A. W. Lee (1905) *(Figure 88)*, a civilized barbarian who refused to accept his portrait, but paid

86. JOHN GEST
1905. 40 x 30. Fidelity-Philadelphia Trust Company.

Eakins for it and returned it to him. Eakins' view of him contains that kind of response. His portrait may appear one of Eakins' most harsh revelations of character, omitting nothing in its delineation of the stiff and the inhuman, from the rigidity of the man's pose to the marmoreal quality of his long face with its hard gray-blue eyes. Yet inhumanity is not all one discovers in the man, for what had frozen in him, after all, was a superior energy. If he could not like what Eakins found in him others may be struck by the sheer power of vision in this intense work, and by something that competes with that stiff probity, that angry response to life. Lee's eyes are not simply hard; they hint at the beginnings of self-recognition, the discovery that life had been lost in the pursuit of something else. This work belongs to moral vision, but it communicates its impression with a richness that has its sources in the response to an era and in the ability to probe the psychology of a most unlikely subject.

IN 1904, Frank Stokes secured a portrait commission for his old teacher from Robert Ogden, a merchant. Once more the completed full-length, life-size work *(Figure 89)* did not please the sitter; Ogden offered to return it after paying for it but Eakins would not accept it. Ogden preserved the painting, perhaps feeling that he had too much in it to destroy it. And the portrait may strike the uninitiated even today as simply hard and, like the Lee, in a tradition of unimaginative realism, the portrait of a man in a black suit, the details of his clothing hardly distinguishable, his left leg crossed over his right, his formidable black shoe placed squarely on the oriental rug. Ogden is seated upright again almost rigidly, in a Hepplewhite chair, the right hand resting on the chair's arm, only the wrist of the left hand showing beyond his crossed left leg. The chair and the rug are turned diagonally to the horizontal line of the wall behind; the light coming from the right falls upon Ogden's face, upon his hands, the rug, and the left side of the painting — especially upon the tapestry behind him, a woodland or a hunting scene. Most of the right side of that tapestry is indistinguishable in its shadow.

The lineaments of psychic and physical power show themselves everywhere in this old merchant prince, in eyes, carriage, in that powerfully highlighted right hand. But Eakins' sense, and Ogden's, of what lies beneath that surface, is what distinguishes this painting in particular and his art in general. The large red ear of some of these portraits is not here; the right ear is not really distinguishable in the shadow. The device forces us to the meaning in his eyes, wide and staring, in the thin-lipped, firm mouth, in the gray, squarely cut beard. Tired, set in the flesh sagging beneath them, yet penetrating, with-

87. CHARLES E. DANA
1902. 50 x 30. Courtesy of The Pennsylvania Academy of the Fine Arts.

88. A. W. LEE
1905. 40 x 32. Lawrence A. Fleischman.

89. ROBERT C. OGDEN
1904. 72 x 48. Joseph H. Hirshhorn Collection.

90. DR. WILLIAM THOMSON
1907. 74 x 48. College of Physicians, Philadelphia.

out illusion, his eyes are also caught in dream, as if the tapestry, half revealed there, were a vaguely troubling reminder of some ungraspable verdant world lost in a past more dim than the light falling upon it. This portrait inevitably reminds me of the last pages of *The Great Gatsby* where Fitzgerald's themes were also the erosions of time and the failure of a dream.

In the 1907 portrait of the physician William Thomson *(Figure 90)* there is nothing like the moral or psychological intensity of the Lee *(Figure 88)* or the Ogden *(Figure 89)*, but there is a profoundly sympathetic response to the man. Thomson is seated in a chair, his left arm resting on a table, his right hand closed in his lap holding an opthalmoscope, his legs crossed. He faces the spectator as he might have faced a patient, objective inquiry and inward reflection both working in that steady look, frowning almost as if he were in physical pain, the eyes simultaneously searching and abstracted, looking down at us through his pince-nez. The old man's collar is loose above the red bow tie; the physical erosion suggested is opposed to the strong hands, a kind of reassurance. The darkened painting has a grandeur, a grave majesty, and something of a ghostly quality — the dimly highlighted head and hands luminous against that somber background, the doctor isolated in time, in age, in memory as he is in space, in a room dominated by the sense of twilight. That portrait is in a way a prophecy as well as a commentary upon an age, for the humanity of this deeply human physician belongs, one may feel, more to the past than to the future.

What comes through at last in these portraits is Eakins' human responsiveness and his expressive force penetrating his subject and refusing to compromise with what he discovers there, yet frequently balancing the old intensity of moral and psychic scrutiny with some wider but no less profound confrontation of mortality. These sitters are all of them involved in their sense of personal time. But they are also men of an era immersed in historical time, and we read the moral history of their era through an intelligence that records the response of these representative men to these kinds of time, in a moment apart from the machinery of a civilization of which they were makers and victims. Forty years before Gérôme had told his students, "Imitation must serve expression or you will remain children." In these late portraits, the people and the things represented have the direct kind of symbolic force in which representation and mature meaning are finally indistinguishable.

13

EAKINS' portraits of Cushing *(Figure 60)* and of McClure Hamilton *(Figure 62)* in the mid-nineties had explored human significance in the life-size standing figure; now in several works at the end of the nineteenth and the beginning of the twentieth centuries he continued to seek individual meanings through this form. Always aware of the weight, the mass, the palpable substance of the human body, that consciousness deepened as he grew older and heavier himself, and the men in these portraits came to appear ever more directly conscious of the weight of plain mortality. Yet Eakins' naturalism was qualified, for biological and psychological truth and the facts of human weariness were seen in tension with this essentially affirmative act of standing.

IN *The Dean's Roll Call (Figure 91)* he recorded, in 1899, an impression that had also been made upon graduating classes of the Jefferson Medical College. They had seen Professor James W. Holland calling the roll of graduates and reading the Hippocratic oath with "almost religious fervor." But his colleagues objected to the Dean's "tense almost haggard expression" in the full-length portrait and refused to buy it. "So Eakins," Holland's son writes, "having no general market at the time . . . as a friendly gesture gave the picture to my mother."

The portrait of Dean Holland was as close to official portraiture as Eakins could make it. The weak-minded men who refused the work objected to as much of the sense of life as they had found in it for there is an unambiguously affirmative force in the portrait, an uncommon vitality and solidity in the robed figure. Dean Holland stands looking up, holding an open folder before him, his fervor all bound up with the ideals of his profession, the haggard

91. THE DEAN'S ROLL CALL
1899. 84 x 42. Museum of Fine Arts, Boston (Abraham Shuman Fund).

92. THE THINKER

1900. 82 x 42. The Metropolitan Museum of Art, Kennedy Fund, 1917.

expression implying a commitment more profound than his colleagues could understand, the man lending as much life to his calling as it gives meaning to his own existence.

A year later (1900) Eakins painted *The Thinker (Figure 92)*, a full-length portait of his brother-in-law Louis Kenton. The title recalls Rodin's heavily muscled romantic nude, but there is no further resemblance between the works. Eakins' *Thinker* creates something like a crisis of personal awareness in the solitary stoical figure, a recognition, one may feel, that now directly takes in a moment of history. Yet the sober man stands against that luminous gray-green background isolated from any object which might symbolize that era, alone, his hands in the pockets of baggy trousers, his eyes cast down and unclear behind his pince-nez. Together, and each in his own way, Eakins and Kenton stand athwart that grain of the American heritage which could see hope in the coming century as something apart from individual human experience. In the worn strength and the integrity of the contemplative man an understanding is affirmed that is apart from hope, and apart, for that matter, from simple resignation. *The Thinker* achieves its generic meaning with a force that loses nothing of Kenton's personal existence. [*See note, page 294.*]

In the early part of this century Charles Sheeler entered the School of Industrial Art in Philadelphia where, he recalled, "One day a stocky little man, gray-haired and gray-bearded, passed through our workroom" to begin a portrait of Leslie Miller, the school's principal. "As the artist's work continued we witnessed the progress of a perspective drawing which was made on paper and then transferred to the canvas. . . . This careful procedure led us to the conclusion that the man, whoever he was, couldn't be a great artist, for we had learned somewhere that great artists painted only by inspiration." A few months later Sheeler watched the artist complete his work and transfer the perspective drawing of a signature to the canvas. "The letters spelled Eakins. The name was not familiar to us." [*See note, page 294.*]

The portrait of Miller (1901) *(Figure 93)* had some success in its time, winning a prize in the 1905 exhibition of the National Academy of Design. Whether the climate was changing, or whether the painting seemed to take its subject by main force in a substantial, old-fashioned way, the jury responded to this vision of the professional man seen in isolation, a heavy, weary figure who eyes the spectator directly, his manuscript in one hand, his other hand in his pocket. The pose contains its energy and yet is physically

93. PROFESSOR LESLIE MILLER
1901. 88⅛ x 44. Collection of the Philadelphia Museum of Art.

94. PROFESSOR WILLIAM SMITH FORBES
1905. 84 x 48. Jefferson Medical College, Philadelphia.

and intellectually aggressive and the seemingly static design contributes to this effect. Miller stands before a brownish-orange screen, above and behind which is a darker wall. To the left of the screen is another wall running diagonally backward, the school's charts of design painted in perspective on them. The angles of screen and walls have the effect of thrusting Miller forward while he stands in that felt space, back from the picture plane, isolated, bearing his own monumental weight. The dynamic quality of the stance itself is in the gesture of the heavy right hand, and in the direct gray-blue eyes. Using the most ordinary human materials in this large canvas, the heavy graying lecturer in his old clothes, Eakins merged his naturalistic and his symbolic meanings to affirm a force of character existing beyond disappointment and disillusion, a human understanding still grounded in the weight of body, of mortal human experience itself, and an aggressive intelligence encompassing that experience and that life.

THERE are human victories in each of these paintings yet they are never blatantly announced. In them the old, grave subtleties take on their most forthright shapes, but they are shapes in which life is still at issue. Their effects are hardly exciting in any superficial way, but they can be profoundly moving. One of the late standing figures, done in 1905, is that of William Smith Forbes *(Figure 94)* who was seventy-four when Eakins painted him lecturing in an amphitheater at the Jefferson Medical College. The fingers of the old man's open left hand rest on a pedestal table near a copy of "The Anatomy Act of Pennsylvania" he had drawn up some forty years before, a book, and a skull. He is a portly man, nearly bald, with white moustaches, and heavy yet sensitive old man's hands. Old echoes haunt this painting: behind Forbes are a group of medical students whose presence recalls the communal theme of *The Agnew Clinic (Figure 43)* and the audience of *The Gross Clinic (Figure 22)*. But this aged man is not dramatically related to the nine students on the benches. There is in him no assertion of intellect or of energy in the ordinary sense; the author of "The Anatomy Act" stands alone with his achievement and with his mortal history, an isolated moral presence.

Eakins' brush is unusually free in this work, his sympathies fully engaged as he communicates the uncertainty of this man's life, the plain burden of its weight, compassionately granting Forbes every enduring quality of character the man possessed, while recording the slowing of his life and intellect. The wing collar, the bow tie, the watch, the chain, the formal coat, the highly polished shoes are the lineaments of character, an old-fashioned decorum in response to duty, a lifetime of honorable devotion to vocation. And honor, thus honestly isolated and honestly seen, has never found more human expression. The portrait of Forbes faces that of Benjamin Howard Rand *(Figure 10)*, across the stairwell, painted in another mood thirty years before.

14

IN the early years of the century Samuel Murray introduced Eakins to a number of members of the Catholic hierarchy at St. Charles Seminary in Overbrook. Eakins and his young friend would bicycle out to the Seminary on Sunday and stay to dinner. There, it is said, he could indulge his passion for Latin, and possibly for conversation less provincial than the kind practiced in Philadelphia.

Eakins was an atheist, with a profound distaste for supernatural religion. In pursuing his acquaintance with men of intellect and distinction he was behaving out of his very civilized habit and not out of any newly discovered religious necessity. These men represented connections to broader cultural and aesthetic traditions than were generally recognized in Philadelphia. He was also drawn to them because they were outsiders, men like himself, apart from the mainstream of life in Philadelphia and from the currents of twentieth-century American civilization.

He took the opportunity to paint a group of these churchmen, requesting most of them to pose, receiving commissions from several others. It was a chance to relate himself to one of the great traditions of Western portraiture, one that had produced psychological studies of great power three and four centuries before. By painting them in their vestments he could exploit possibilities of form and sometimes of color not available to him in the dark suits of Philadelphia businessmen. His interest in them was at a tangent to what had become a central strain in his work, the discovery of the tensions and pressures of civilization in the faces of his sitters. Their distance from the recognizable centers of power and from the ordinary concerns of that civilization was a difficulty and a challenge. He responded to the challenge in

95. STUDY FOR PORTRAIT OF ARCHBISHOP JAMES FREDERICK WOOD
1876. 16 x 12⅛. Yale University Art Gallery, bequest of Stephen C. Clark.

96. ARCHBISHOP JAMES FREDERICK WOOD
1877. 82 x 60. St. Charles Seminary, Overbrook.

ways peculiar to him, and produced the most important group of works of this sort ever painted in America.

ALTHOUGH Eakins had painted a religious subject a quarter of a century before, the careful sketch and large seated figure of Archbishop Wood *(Figures 95 and 96)* had not helped him to find other commissions of the same sort. [*See note, page 294.*] The earliest of the group painted after 1900, Eakins' friend Monsignor James Turner *(Figure 97)* is, as pure painting, in some ways the most remarkable. It is the portrait of a man in a cassock, a bald man with a pince-nez who looks meditatively out at the spectator, his hand held to the left side of the face. Sensitivity of response alone never achieved greater impact in an Eakins portrait; one feels it here in the modeling of the hand, in the recording of gesture, and in the quiet tonal qualities, the variations of gray which help to establish the painting's mood. Responding to the sensibility of a man whose personality was rich and open to impression, Eakins fashioned a portrait whose vitality appears out of all proportion to its means. This effect, not entirely rare in his work — the taciturnity of expression, the economy of means employed to achieve a strong impression — is one of the sources of his distinctive power in that difficult form, the head-and-bust portrait.

Several other heads and busts may appear more prosaic than the Turner, but each conveys its distinct effect. In the portrait, painted in 1902, of the Rector of St. Charles Seminary, Patrick Garvey *(Figure 98)*, there is pain in the eyes of a man whose features otherwise express strength and solidity. [*See note, page 294.*] There is also something approaching anguish in the expression of James A. Flaherty *(Figure 99)*, a layman, Supreme Knight of the Order of the Knights of Columbus, whom Eakins painted in 1903. But the portrait has another sort of movement, for at a distance Flaherty is very much an old-fashioned Philadelphia type, and Eakins, reminded also of Bismarck, must have delighted in taking his likeness on that account alone. Finally, the head and bust of the Rt. Rev. Denis (later Cardinal) Dougherty (1903) *(Figure 100)* is a reading of a complex personality. His eyes, though obscured by his glasses, convey a strength, almost a hardness underlying the introspective aspect. And there is something uncommon in those features: a distinct force, a guarded self-consciousness, an unmistakable if veiled intelligence lies behind them. Pain or anguish tempers that expression less than some intensity of purpose.

One of the better known of these works takes the contemplative seriousness of a scholar for its subject to produce its direct and unambiguous impression. In the portrait of Monsignor Hugh Henry, *The Translator (Figure 101)*, painted in 1902, the scholar looks up with a benign, untroubled expression confronting the observer directly, a figure of solidity and strength. He rests his strong hands on a heavy tiger-striped table and this table, the pen he holds, the ink pot, the book, the portrait of a smiling Leo XIII in the background (more interesting in this version by Eakins than in the original down the hallway) are all assimilated to a vision that reminds us of Manet, of Velásquez, of Rembrandt. The painting uses light and shadow to increase the effect of a sculptural solidity strangely, for Eakins, apart from time. In that arrested moment of meditation there is a quality of permanence beyond mortality. There is no skull on the table, no hint of Vanitas. *The Translator* is among the least complex of the Catholic portraits in the sense it establishes of cloistered virtue in a warm library room, but, like the Turner, it is among the most painterly.

Yet at its best Eakins' imagination demanded more complex human possibility in the men he painted. The fullest powers of his human insight were most deeply engaged when Cardinal Martinelli sat for him in 1902. The life-size full-length portrait of the Cardinal *(Figure 102)* assaults the observer with the strength and the intensity of its appeal. This large faded thinly painted canvas is the most powerful portrait of its kind ever painted by an American.

The Cardinal is seated in a high-backed ornate chair looking into the light, and the impression is of physical and intellectual tension in a moment of coercive restraint. That effect is focused in the Cardinal's intent eyes, in all the subtle rendering of the keen, the quick, the penetrating. There is strength in the face caught in light, in the forehead and strong nose, in the firm mouth and chin, in every element of that so powerfully conceived head. And the painting's effect, of extraordinary life rendered, of life extraordinarily conveyed, is communicated again by the hands, the right on the arm of the chair, the left holding the Cardinal's hat; these are neither objectively sensitive nor innately remarkable, but they are so expressively rendered that they startlingly evoke their subtle complementary meanings — one at rest, the other so negligently holding the symbol of rank.

The impression of force and of counterforce is as much in the design of the work as in the Cardinal's figure itself, and especially in the space about the body. The perspective manages to convey a sense of energy, of body almost thrust out upon us, yet remaining very much there in that dark.

97. MSGR. JAMES P. TURNER
About 1900. 24 x 20. St. Charles Seminary, Overbrook.

98. RT. REV. MSGR. PATRICK J. GARVEY
1902. 24 x 20. St. Charles Seminary, Overbrook.

99. JAMES A. FLAHERTY
1903. 27 x 22. St. Charles Seminary, Overbrook.

100. RT. REV. DENIS J. DOUGHERTY
1903. 24 x 20. Mr. and Mrs. Harry F. Boylan.

101. THE TRANSLATOR
1902. 50 x 40. St. Charles Seminary, Overbrook.

102. CARDINAL MARTINELLI
1902. 79¼ x 60. Catholic University of America.

paneled room, enclosed and isolated. It is as if the man in his pride and strength were reflecting in this moment not, paradoxically, upon himself, but upon the Church which grants him power, and which diminishes him and includes him. It is a very civilized Renaissance prince we see here.

The portrait of Archbishop Elder of Cincinnati *(Figure 103)*, painted in 1903, later won a gold medal at the Pennsylvania Academy. There were no ambiguities in Eakins' response to the moral and intellectual qualities of this man, rather something approaching forthright admiration for the rich preservation of humanity in one so old. Archbishop Elder's seeming awareness of his own mortality is one of the painting's strongest notes. Eakins' sense of the aged body beneath the vestments reflects the Archbishop's awareness of himself, and the meditative quality of the portrait is associated with the impression of physical frailty. But its direct appeal lies even more in its understated perception of the plain virtue of endurance apprehended as strength of character in an exceptional man opposing inexorable time.

Eakins, it is said, thought it "a heap of impudence" for the Academy to award him a gold medal for this portrait. To Eakins the Academy was still an unclean object, still genteel Philadelphia stinking of Sunday piety whose approbation was more than a simple insult. And so, the story goes, he rode over on bicycle in a costume meant to disturb those decent people, claimed his medal, and dropped it off at the Mint on his way back to Mt. Vernon Street.

In *Monsignor Diomede Falconio* (1905) *(Figure 104)* rich brown tones dominate the portrait of a heavier, older man seated on a dais. Again there is strength in hands and face though the sitter has neither the intellectual nor the emotional force of Cardinal Martinelli, nor the depth of humanity of Archbishop Elder. It is his stolidity, the conveyed sense of a blunt humanity not without its own kind of understanding that physically dominates this space, and his isolation is as apart from any projected sense of physical frailty as it is from personal pride. This is the last of these powerful seated figures of Catholic clergymen. It defines the form in some absolute way, with a sculptural solidity, a directness, a bluntness that must have been perfect complements of the Monsignor's character.

In the life-size portraits of laymen, Eakins usually associated the act of standing with some sort of victory of character. The standing figure of a clergyman did not always produce an impression of that sort. He painted

103. ARCHBISHOP WILLIAM HENRY ELDER
1903. 66¼ x 45½. The Archdiocese of Cincinnati.

104. MSGR. DIOMEDE FALCONIO
1905. 72 x 54⅜. National Gallery of Art, Washington, D.C.,
Gift of Stephen C. Clark.

a large full-length portrait of Monsignor James Loughlin *(Figure 105)* in 1902 on inferior canvas, possibly on burlap, which deteriorated radically over the years. Recently restored, the work is demonstrably an Eakins, but one in which the act of standing is no more than that. The work may have been totally uninspired.

The portrait of Father Fedigan *(Figure 106)* at Villanova College, which is nearly in its original condition, is also more demonstrably affirmative in its view. Standing in his black cassock, his left forearm resting on a stand bearing a picture of a building and the inscription "Monastery of St. Thomas, Villa Nova," his face sculptural, almost lean in contrast to the weight of his body, Father Fedigan shows himself a person of contained physical and emotional force. There is no complex human insight in this large gray work. Its mood is as gray as its tone but it implies no anguish. Father Fedigan is a figure of epic in a painting which avoids any inflation of the epic effect.

For anything approaching the complexity or the intensity of the Cardinal Martinelli work one must wait until the end of this cycle, until 1906, for the second portrait of Monsignor Turner *(Figure 107)* now seen standing before the high altar in the Cathedral of Sts. Peter and Paul, his hands clasped before him, holding a book. The floor of the Cathedral, the alternating black and gray squares of marble, produces a sense of isolating space in tension with the almost felt contact the priest makes with the observer. His searching stare, simultaneously more probing and more introspective than the earlier portrait, is reminiscent of those direct confrontations one encounters in the late head and bust portraits. Though one may argue that this large painting has its very special enigmatic effect because it has darkened, or because it is poorly lighted in its hallway at the Misericordia Hospital, it is an effect conveyed at last by something in the man himself, by his complex humanity, by the self-questioning that appears to extend beyond himself as he stands there, whether he is officiating at a service or standing alone in an empty Cathedral.

Today it is difficult to disassociate these paintings from the places in which one finds them, a hallway in the library of the Catholic University, the longer, darker hallway of the main building at St. Charles Seminary, a stair landing in the library at Villanova University, a dark cul-de-sac in Misericordia Hospital. Nothing to match them has ever been painted in this country, but in those hallways their special quality may remain rather elusive, inextricably involved as it is with Eakins' old quality of restraint, finding such singular

105. MSGR. JAMES F. LOUGHLIN
1902. 90 x 45. St. Charles Seminary, Overbrook.

106. VERY REV. JOHN J. FEDIGAN
1902. Detail. 89½ x 50. Villanova College.

107. MSGR. JAMES P. TURNER
1906. 88 x 42. Misericordia Hospital, Philadelphia.

expression here. Restraint shows itself so consistently in his view of these men that one may be inclined to feel the group expresses nothing so much as his good manners, his affable willingness to mitigate, in the face of these decent representatives of the Church, the sort of scrutiny he exercised in other later work when he laid bare the moral or psychic anatomy of a layman distinguished by intelligence or by energy, by an accomplishment or by a pretension that was out of the ordinary. Yet he neither sought nor could he discover the same kind of malaise in different kinds of men; here, the special humanity of the dedicated priest is his subject, the special humanity of men who by their vocation had placed themselves apart from the currents of American history and from the uncertainties of the new century, but not from the human condition. The portraits discover ranges of human response, from anguish and doubt to stolid certainty, from the introspection of Monsignor Turner, to the worldly sagacity and human decency of Archbishop Elder; from the almost surprised abstraction of the translator, to the plain power and contained force of Cardinal Martinelli. There is not a forced note among them and there is no display. The portraits achieve their subtle effects with an economy of paint and through simplicities of design and restraints of statement that argue no magnificence. They are Eakins seemingly at his most unimpassioned, observing quietly, employing no rhetoric, creating, through the great force of his reserve, their paradoxical and unmistakable splendor.

15

To be the child of one's time.
Naturalism against your own self.
Objectivity of the inner vision.
— Max Beckmann

EAKINS had, in the portraits of three decades, explored feminine consciousness from premises with which his civilization was not superficially in disagreement. If he saw them as more sensitive and more given to moody introspection than men, nineteenth-century portraitists were quite as willing to grant as much. He moved beyond the work of others through his refusal to idealize beauty in the manner of more fashionable portraitists, by his disregard of the necessity to remake the public image of elegance and modesty in each successive portrait, and through his willingness and his ability to discover human meanings either unavailable to or avoided by lesser minds. Character fascinated him, and submerged personality. Honesty was essential if one were to do justice to either, but honesty was only a tool of his total perception, a function of other kinds of awareness.

The portrait sketch of Miss Emily Sartain *(Figure 69)* had foreshadowed his later attention to an image of woman that had not appeared in his work before, that of the aging matriarch in whom strength of character is seen in tension with some of the era's characteristic repressions. Again he created no stereotypes; these women in their moments of recognition assert their powerful individual claims to life in new and surprising ways.

Among these studies of matriarchs is the 1900 portrait of Mrs. Frishmuth *(Figure 108)*, measuring eight by six feet, nearly as large as *The Gross Clinic*, and one of the splendid achievements of his last decade. The painting has a massive force, a grandeur and a power that take their vitality from a complex response to character, and perhaps from a complex character herself. Mrs. Frishmuth, a collector of musical instruments and honorary curator of musical

108. MRS. WILLIAM D. FRISHMUTH
1900. 96 x 72. Collection of the Philadelphia Museum of Art.

instruments at the Pennsylvania Museum, surrounded by the symbols of her special sensitivity, holds on her lap a tenor viol, an English viola d'amore. Symbols of formidable strength and of an ornate, arcane delicacy alternate with one another, Mrs. Frishmuth and her instruments, the instruments and one another, the peacock vina, the small bagpipes and the pianoforte, the Lama horn and a mysterious drum. There are other bagpipes, cymbals, pipes of Pan, drums, and an unidentified duck-shaped instrument; in the right foreground, an organistrum with a crank; in the corner, an upturned lute signed "Eakins." There is a pattern of design in this arrangement, and possibly a dark humor in the symbolism. The instruments lying in the foreground give space to that room: generally they are pointed diagonally inward and to the right, toward the horn and drum in the dark background.

The effect of the painting is rooted in the enigma of a personality. Mrs. Frishmuth and her collection are mysteries; she is a powerful, remarkably unlovely upright woman with a hard face and a meditative stare who dominates the space about her as she presses a single key of the pianoforte with one finger of her right hand and tunes the instrument in her lap. The gesture is simultaneously realistic and a conceit; no sound wakens Mrs. Frishmuth from her trance.

This heavy-necked, square-faced lady with her blue neckerchief, her delicate pearls and her black dress must have had some faith in Eakins to sit for him for as long as he required, and he, in his turn, evidently thought her worthy of his massive effort. We do not know what she made of her portrait. If it did justice to her strength of character and to her collection, she might well have objected to the frozen presentation of so much of the rest of her. But I also suspect that she was unaware of the restrained, the slumbering spirit of Rabelais beneath the surface of this sober vision of herself as grand matriarch holding a viol of love in her lap. Raphael was there before Eakins came, but Mrs. Frishmuth is the image of a Victorian St. Cecilia that Raphael could not have conjured.

THE deep resentment of the life-distorting forces of genteel society which had frustrated him for a lifetime showed itself in small eccentricities of dress his friends remarked upon. At one time or another he wore his corduroy breeches, his flannel shirt, his pea jacket and his carpet slippers upon inappropriate occasions. He wore the gray knee breeches with a sailor hat, or a heavy white pullover, sailor cap, and white pants as he cycled about Philadelphia. It is said that when the Academy of Fine Arts decided to exhibit

109. MRS. ELIZABETH DUANE GILLESPIE

1901. 45 x 30. Collection of the Women's Committee of the Philadelphia Museum of Art.

his *Between Rounds* after rejecting it for ten years, Eakins, in his mid-sixties, appeared for the showing on a high-wheeled bicycle, wearing red bicycle pants, thus repeating the impression he had made when accepting the gold medal for his portrait of Archbishop Elder.

This all has reference to the powerful Mrs. Gillespie *(Figure 109)*, whom he posed in the hot summer of 1901 in the heat of his studio, wearing, one supposes, his undershirt and carpet slippers out of deference to her. Mrs. Gillespie was the great-granddaughter of Benjamin Franklin and she was offended. How did she decide to sit for him? Leslie Miller may have recommended him, and she may well have known little or nothing of Eakins' history. Besides, she was a strong-minded person, a power in the social world of Philadelphia who had displayed courage over a long lifetime and she might easily have been willing to risk the encounter for a superior result. She had been matron of a hospital for the wounded during the Civil War, and later President of the Women's Executive Committee of the 1876 Exhibition, in which role she was largely responsible for getting the Exhibition on its feet. During the Exhibition she was accused of being narrow and bigoted, and of having excluded two women from exhibiting whose accomplishments were glories to their sex — Mrs. Maxwell, huntress and naturalist of Colorado, and Mrs. Brossie, the only woman miner in the world. She survived these accusations, and she survived in Eakins' powerful unfinished portrait of her, another matriarch of that era, facing the world directly, her strong hands before her, in a plain black dress. She looks outward and her expression admits to no sense of failure in the world. In Mrs. Gillespie Eakins saw the sensitivities and insensitivities of a response to existence in which fortitude and a cold assessment of reality are written large. The virtues and the repressions of the age are written in the hardened features of the older woman, an American historical fact.

He very nearly finished this impressive work even though Mrs. Gillespie refused to return to his attic studio after the episode of the undershirt. Eakins' response to her is of great interest, for although she was the momentary representative of the narrow power of the genteel, there is no rancor in his vision. On the contrary, the portrait projects his admirations for the felt qualities of her character, and a sadness, a regret for the effects of this life's campaign.

The portrait of Mrs. Gilbert Lafayette Parker *(Figure 110)* painted almost a decade later, in 1910, marks in its way the end of an age. This grande

110. MRS. GILBERT LAFAYETTE PARKER
1910. 24 x 20. Courtesy, Museum of Fine Arts, Boston (Charles Henry Hayden Fund).

dame, the last of Eakins' matriarchs, is another incarnation of moral force staring out at the world in penetrating appraisal. Her right eyelid droops and her flesh sags, but there is a strength in her features — in the eyes, the firm mouth, the strong neck. The light is full on the right side of that formidable head. "[It] has as much mellowness in its color, as much ease in its stroke, as he ever allowed himself," a critic wrote of this painting. "Yet the pinkish skin and the bluish eyes glow from the dull brown and faded gold of the dress and background with an internal light which seems to be the very will to live, without assistance from the sensuous qualities of the outside world." In disregard or even in defiance of them one might say, for there is a fierce quality in Mrs. Parker, an assertion of individuality that will not be downed. The rapid brushwork in the handling of her dress may be a sign of Eakins' great physical fatigue, that weariness which gripped him in the last years of his life, but the free use of the brush which he would not have permitted to stand as finished in an earlier work is very effective here. The dark dress and high collar are emblems of a spirit that played its own role in that age. Once more Eakins discovers the intense individuality within the type, and something curiously like admiration for the type herself, the Victorian woman whose strength, judgment, and whose narrowness characterized important areas of the civilization he had known.

He continued of course to be interested in women for the reasons that had always moved him, for their beauty, for the sense of the individual consciousness responding to life and he found one of his great subjects in a friend, Signora Enrico Gomez D'Arza, an Italian actress, the wife of a poor impressario of a small theater in the Italian section of South Philadelphia. *Signora Gomez D'Arza* (1902) *(Figure 111)*, a classic portrait whose intimations of the tragic are handled with the greatest restraint, reveals a woman whose full staring eyes (her left in shadow as the light strikes the right side of her face) appear to take in all the strength and illusion of youth, and the impossible twistings of that dream. She wears an elaborate full-sleeved lace-trimmed Spanish costume (symbol of the dream more than of an era), a reflection, in a quiet theatrical way, of the uncommon elevated spirit of the tragic heroine. She leans slightly forward in her chair, her attitude and her brooding face marking a distance from hope and belief, that is, mysteriously, beyond despair. Light and shadow contain these meanings as well as the human forms themselves, the shape of the mouth, the right hand at rest . . . The painting reminds one of the great Spanish masters and yet, I think, only

111. SIGNORA GOMEZ D'ARZA
1902. 30 x 24. The Metropolitan Museum of Art, George A. Hearn Fund, 1927.

112. MRS. MARY HALLOCK GREENEWALT
1903. 36 x 24. Wichita Art Museum, Roland P. Murdock Collection, Wichita, Kansas.

113. MRS. EDITH MAHON
1904. 20 x 16. Smith College Museum of Art.

a profound modern consciousness could have painted it. Despair has been encompassed not by faith but by a mysterious and astonishing art.

MARY HALLOCK GREENEWALT, a concert pianist, was thirty-two when Eakins painted her three-quarter-length portrait *(Figure 112)* in 1903, a woman with black hair held fairly closely to her head, wearing a low-cut lilac evening dress that revealed her bare neck, chest, and arms. She wears a bracelet on the wrist of her left hand, the right hand beneath it, caught in shadow. The posed gesture has a dynamic stillness. Mrs. Greenewalt holds her forearms down and before her; the hands do not touch.

This portrait moves us as almost no other Eakins portrait of a woman does (one thinks back to the very different portrait of Elizabeth, then to the more nearly comparable portrait of his wife) by the very directness of its confrontation, its challenge. Eakins has emphasized the anatomy of face and neck, discovering the significance of bone structure and taut musculature, sculpting the planes of the face especially, lean and hard in one aspect, to produce the sense of an austere almost masculine quality in tension with a profoundly sensuous and feminine nature. The woman lives in gesture and in the depth of those remarkable eyes, fixing the spectator with their bold assertion of life, holding us by her scrutiny, making her vital claim upon us, compelling response. [*See note, page 294.*]

This self-assurance of the woman who remains a woman while taking in her world and measuring it without illusion is not what struck him when he painted another pianist, Edith Mahon, in 1904 *(Figure 113)*. Mrs. Mahon is entirely feminine in the projected quality of her deep sensitivity, but her eyes, turned away from the spectator, express personal injury and pain in a way that drives all comparisons out of mind. The intense light falling upon face and breast has a quality of the absolute about it, the light in which the entire course of a life is revealed. The demanding economies of the head and bust portrait have never found stronger form than they do here. Restrained anguish and grief have never been more powerfully interpreted.

IN 1908 Eakins posed Miss Helen Parker in a dress that had belonged to Miss Parker's grandmother, calling the three-quarter-length portrait *The Old-Fashioned Dress (Figure 114)*. Miss Parker stands with her arm over the back of the chair he had used to pose his sitters in from Katherine's time on, a sweet dull young woman who stares off in a kind of trance. The girl we see is uncertain of her connection to the past yet she is dominated by it. And it is

114. THE OLD-FASHIONED DRESS
1908. 60⅛ x 40¼. Collection of the Philadelphia Museum of Art.

not recognition but the failure of understanding in one so young that we read in that face. She had been disconcerted while posing because he would not make her "just a little pretty." "You're very beautiful. You're very beautiful," he reassured her, while attending to the inner vision.

These portraits remind us how far Eakins' art as portraitist stands beyond any simple realism. An ordinary realism might organize its objective data into a scheme recognized and accepted by its audience, perhaps softening its impression, but it would yield before any effort to discover mystery. The interest of genius is greatest, Henry James remarked at about this time, when it commits itself simultaneously in the direction of the romantic and the real. "Of the men of largest responding imagination before the human scene . . . the current remains extraordinarily rich and mixed, washing us successively with the warm wave of the near and familiar and the tonic shock . . . of the far and strange." By the "far and strange" James meant the unknowable. We recall his failure to discover "that adventurous vision of the indefinite" in Copley, and the absence, in Sargent, of that "quality in the light of which the artist sees deep into his subject, undergoes it, absorbs it, discovers in it new things that were not on the surface, becomes patient with it, and almost reverent, and in short, enlarges and humanizes the technical problem."

16

A performance which exceeds expectation, prevision and estimate; sharp edged individuality; defiant opposition to compromise; an attitude of this cannot be otherwise; a spiritual obsession which is akin to madness — these are somewhat obvious characteristics of the genius, which operates outside the conventions of taste of its period, in tragic isolation.

— Max Friedländer

IN an interview granted toward the end of his life Eakins called Winslow Homer the best living American painter. Homer had begun as a lithographer and illustrator and thus came to his subject matter, the treatment of the American scene, quite naturally within a tradition in which it was possible to do honorable work. He was fortunate in that illustration helped him to sharpen his eye, to discover new angles of vision, to develop his sense of design. Then his fame as an illustrator aided his career as painter; he was known, and his more serious work sold. There was much in the American experience as well as in themselves that drove men like Homer, Eakins and Ryder inward. Homer suffered least of them publicly because his objective reputation had been measurably established by the numbers of copies of *Harper's Weekly* in which his work appeared for twenty years.

The isolation of Eakins' sitters corresponded, of course, to his habitual way of seeing as well as to his experience as an artist. Homer could move toward personal isolation while developing new freedoms and new strengths in design and color, in watercolors which avoided the ugly changes in the urban American landscapes and which were unsuited, as the painter was, to any profound handling of the human figure or of individual psychology. In this respect at least he was ironically an artist now firmly in the tradition of American "high art" which in its landscapes and its portraits before the middle of the nineteenth century had tended to avoid significant areas of

115. THE OBOE PLAYER
1903. 36 x 24. Collection of the Philadelphia Museum of Art.

116. A SINGER (MRS. W. H. BOWDEN)
1906. 24 x 20. Leonard Baskin.

American reality. [*See note, page 296.*] Although Eakins differed from Homer as an artist in nearly every important way, their later subject matter and their methods were surely conditioned in some measure by their troubled response to the American experience, for whatever was happening in America drove Homer to those landscapes apart from modern American man, and Eakins to his ever deepening scrutiny of the psyches of the men and women Homer avoided. Eakins' early work in watercolor, however precisely he had handled the medium, could never have expressed the full power and complexity of his vision. In the late portraits he immersed himself in American fact as best he subjectively could through his reading of lives which had taken their final shape in a developing industrial civilization. He was like Homer in his refusal or his inability to look at the landscape of that civilization. He could no more paint his beloved and changing city than Homer could paint New York.

The habits of introspection and scrutiny formed the important psychic elements of his later work transforming the materials of the objective world, the people themselves and the occasional photographs of them into the shape of his personal style. When Eakins used photographs as the basis for some of his work, whatever seemingly objective reality was discovered by the camera was converted to his own way of seeing and feeling. If the photograph could give shape to his design, it took months of sittings to record the unique quality of a personality. Eakins was never bound to the object in any slavish way: he always used it for a purpose which encompassed simple truth to nature. His studies of motion with Muybridge, for instance, appeared to focus not upon motion, but upon stopped motion, an intuition of an aspect of felt time that had been expressed ten years before in the sculling scenes, and then in the late portraits themselves where the sitters are suspended in the changing light of a moment, eternal and unchanging, mortal and dying, the moment of illumination competing with the lifetime of pursuit.

He had painted *The Cello Player (Figure 63)* in 1896, in the midst of that decade of uncertainty, a work whose strength and monumentality are not alone a matter of form, but of his absolute belief in the redeeming power of art. Though Rudolph Hennig lives in his moment, he appears, in his devotion to his art, exempt from time. Similarly, Dr. Benjamin Sharp's mortality was not at issue in *The Oboe Player* (1903) *(Figure 115)*. Part of Eakins' instinctive naturalism, his concern with the biological and psychological effects of time and the era upon his sitters, suspended itself as he pictured the dream or trancelike state of the absorbed performer. The old stresses reappeared

117. MAJOR MANUEL WALDTEUFEL
1907. 24 x 20. French Benevolent Society of Philadelphia.

118. MUSIC
1904. 39½ x 49¾. Albright-Knox Art Gallery, Buffalo, New York.

movingly when the performer was at rest, as in *Mrs. Mahon (Figure 113)*, the unfinished *A Singer* (1906) *(Figure 116)*, or in *Major Waldteufel* (1907) *(Figure 117)* where the violinist, holding his violin in his left hand, shows his heavy mournful sagging face, and probably the saddest large-eyed Gallic gaze ever recorded. (I can only speak of this work with affection.) In *Music* (1904) *(Figure 118)* all these signs of anguish disappear again as movement and time itself are suspended — in the opposed diagonals of violin and bow, in the pyramidal design of the work — but more, in the mind of the artist who conceives the creative moment as one of timeless ritual. [*See note, page 296.*]

Something like this feeling underlies the late *William Rush* (1908) *(Figure 119)* where all the sensuous color of the early work is washed out in favor of the tones of brown which envelop the scene in an atmosphere of dream and of myth. The return to the Rush theme after thirty years was more than mere obsession, and more than a sign of a narrowed imagination which could not create other uses for the nude. The Rush "Myth" contained all that Eakins needed, an opportunity to paint body, a chance to reaffirm a validating tradition, and to say what he had meant to say on a scale more nearly proper to the intended monumental and epic effect. There is a ritual stillness in the figures of the Negro chaperone, the model and the sculptor as he works upon the figure of a goddess, seeking beauty in an ordinary, even somewhat heavy woman's body, and in some idea beyond body, as Eakins always had. His brush moves broadly, sensitively, confidently: more realistic than the early painting, this work is yet more mysterious in its perception and revelation of the creative act.

PHOTOGRAPHS taken during the last years of his life record the tired, brooding face, flesh and consciousness itself sagging under some impossible weight. He and Samuel Murray were said to have been poisoned by milk illegally dosed with formaldehyde used as a preservative; whether or not that actually happened, he had labored under the stresses of increasing psychic and physical exhaustion; an accumulation of toxins had sapped his will and eaten away at him psychically over the years and these were bound to show their effect. He had more recognition during the last decade of his work than he had known all the years before, but it came too late. [*See note, page 296.*] His great strength, grounded in his relationship to his father and in the craftsmanly tradition he had inherited, in standards which no one but the artist himself could question, had been continually assaulted, degraded, forced into nar-

119. WILLIAM RUSH CARVING HIS ALLEGORICAL FIGURE OF THE SCHUYLKILL RIVER

1908. 36 x 48. Courtesy of the Brooklyn Museum.

rower channels. Yet he had endured; he managed to continue painting, not without bitterness, but avoiding an ultimately destructive self-doubt. Bent to the will of larger forces he did not compromise his art.

He had no great students. No one came to him with the broadness of culture or the psychic depth in the teaching years who might have used the human figure as he thought it had to be used, as the basis for some serious and provocative vision of human existence. Who could combine, as he had, the dignity of the great Spaniard, the paganism of a Renaissance Italian, and the meditative quality of the great Dutchman? The student closest to him was Samuel Murray, but Murray had no great talent.

In the last portraits it is as if Eakins meant to coerce beauty from the most recalcitrant materials, from the most austere uses of form. It was no mere exercise of the will, for we have seen how his imagination worked itself out not only in the discovery of the tensions, the opposed possibilities and the ambiguities of character, but in the significance of pose and gesture newly apprehended, these along with color, forming designs that reveal as much about him as about his sitters. The head and bust is the most difficult, the most challenging of the portrait forms. Any failure of technique, of imagination or of insight is sure to show itself there; it must be perfect in its way if it is to be taken seriously; and its perfection will always be inseparable from the human insight and the responding imagination of the painter.

In probing individual human consciousness during the last decade of his work he achieved as much certainty as any painter can hope for in limning the broad, the universal meanings of an eye, of a gaze, of an expression, and of simultaneously implying individuality, difference, significance in the person before him. His realism and his naturalism were always given force by his deeply subjective response to his subjects and by what was always in effect a romanticism, implying that whatever happened to it, spirit was supremely important, spirit supremely mattered. Character, formed classically along the hard lines of the American experience, had still always a mystery about it. He discovered human dignity in ways which distressed his sitters, assessing their humanity out of a total commitment to the best values of a humanistic tradition. His particular authenticity and his moving example lie in his refusal to abandon that tradition as he understood it, and in his adaptation of it to the course of human discovery that was both chosen and forced upon him.

Does his art appear irrelevant in this time when artists fashion impersonal statements to assert their individuality and their freedom? Eakins' art leads in general to intellect and not to its abandonment; to feeling associated with human consciousness in a moment of recognition, and not to feeling or energy asserting itself apart from men. The tension in his work as a whole was always between the concern for body, for strength, dignity, nobility, even loveliness when they showed themselves in their uncommon ways, and his feeling for consciousness, which had revealed itself, in the earlier work, in the interconnection between body, space, light, atmosphere. In some of the late portraits one feels both Eakins and his sitters maturely confronting something like the condition of existential despair, mature in that these confrontations take place in the fullness of life, when transcendence is out of the question but endurance is the chosen necessity, when shipwreck appears an irrevocable state to be faced by the deepest reserves of character. It is not the confrontation of youth with difficulty but of intelligence with fate. His consciousness drew its affirmation from the most sober possible view of life. It is in general not in tune with much of the regressive art of our time which chooses the mindless and the infantile as ways of approaching contemporary existence.

EAKINS' life and his art stand apart from the large objective drift of American civilization and of American history. [*See note, page 296.*] His portraits measure the human consequences of that drift. He reminds us of something we have lost. In our time the house in which Walt Whitman set up and printed *Leaves of Grass* has been torn down. Whitman's house in Camden has been preserved because Mickle Street lies in a valley of ashes near a railroad embankment. Across the river the Eakins house still stands because no developer values that area around Mt. Vernon Street.

In 1913, Eakins had begun a full-length standing portrait of Dr. Edward Spitzka *(Figure 120)*, a professor of anatomy at Jefferson Medical College known for his work on the human brain. He blocked in the masses of the head as Cezanne might have, but he could not go on. His sight was failing and his hand had become unsteady. He died at one o'clock in the morning of June 25, 1916, some four months after Henry James, another sort of exile, had encountered, at last, "the distinguished thing." Both deaths were submerged in prevailing calamity, in the news of fresh disaster.

Like Dr. Samuel Gross, Eakins believed in cremation. His belief in body did not extend to the grave. Nevertheless, his ashes were taken from the house on Mt. Vernon Street and buried with those of his wife after her death in 1938. Woodland Cemetery in West Philadelphia stands on a height above

120. DR. EDWARD ANTHONY SPITZKA
1913. Unfinished; cut down from the original. 30 x 25. Joseph H. Hirshhorn Collection.

the Schuylkill River which flows green and brown and gray, and moves in the wind stirring the few old trees and the few new ones. At the bottom of the hill are the railroad tracks, black against the black embankment. Beyond is the landscape of wires and water tanks, and the parking lots across the river. A worn angel kneels over the grave of Frances Eakins. The graves of Caroline and Margaret are marked with small round-topped stones. The white stones weather poorly and the legends are almost lost. No stone marks the grave of Susan and Thomas Eakins.

Other Paintings by
THOMAS EAKINS

121. JOHN BIGLEN IN A SINGLE SCULL
1874. 24 x 16. Yale University Art Gallery, Whitney Collection of Sporting Art, given by Francis P. Garvan.

122. OARSMEN ON THE SCHUYLKILL
1873. 27 x 47½. The Brooklyn Museum.

123. THE OARSMEN (THE SCHREIBER BROTHERS)
1874. 15 x 22. From the Collection of Mr. and Mrs. John Hay Whitney.

124. SAILING

1874. 32 x 46⅜. Philadelphia Museum of Art, Alex Simpson, Jr. Collection.

125. THE ZITHER PLAYER
1876. Watercolor. 10¾ x 8. Courtesy of The Art Institute of Chicago, Olivia Shaler Swan Memorial Collection.

126. GENERAL GEORGE CADWALADER
1879-1880. $38\frac{1}{2}$ x $24\frac{1}{2}$. The Butler Institute of American Art.

127. DRAWING THE SEINE

1882. Watercolor. 8 x 11. Courtesy of the John G. Johnson Collection, Philadelphia.

128. THE MEADOWS, GLOUCESTER, N. J.
About 1882. 32¼ x 45¼. Collection of the Philadelphia Museum of Art.

129. PROFESSIONALS AT REHEARSAL
About 1883. 16 x 12. Philadelphia Museum of Art: John D. McIlhenny Collection.

130. ARTHUR B. FROST
About 1884. 27 x 22. Collection of the Philadelphia Museum of Art.

131. PROFESSOR WILLIAM D. MARKS
1886. 76 x 54. Collection Washington University, St. Louis.

132. THE BLACK FAN (MRS. TALCOTT WILLIAMS)
1891. Unfinished. 80¼ x 40. Collection of the Philadelphia Museum of Art.

133. LUCY LEWIS
About 1897. 22 x 27⅛. Seymour Adelman.

134. LOUIS HUSSON
1899. 24 x 20. National Gallery of Art, Washington, D.C.
Gift of Katharine Husson Horstick.

135. DAVID WILSON JORDAN
1899. 60¾ x 28¼. Joseph H. Hirshhorn Collection.

136. DR. EDWARD J. NOLAN
About 1900. 24 x 20. Collection of the Philadelphia Museum of Art.

137. HENRY O. TANNER
About 1900. 24⅛ x 20¼. Hyde Collection, Glens Falls, New York.

138. JOHN J. BORIE
Ca. 1896–1900. Unfinished. 80 x 42. Dartmouth College Museum of Art.

139. REV. PHILIP R. McDEVITT
1901. 20 x 16. University Art Gallery, University of Notre Dame,
Gift of Mary R. and Helen C. McDevitt.

140. CHARLES F. HASELTINE
About 1901. 24 x 20. Collection of the Montclair Art Museum.

141. THE YOUNG MAN (KERN DODGE)
About 1902. Unfinished. 45 x 26. Collection of the Philadelphia Museum of Art.

142. WILLIAM B. KURTZ
1903. 52 x 32. William Fulton Kurtz.

143. MISS ALICE KURTZ
1903. 24 x 20. Mrs. John B. Whiteman.

144. THE ACTRESS
1903. 80 x 59½. Collection of the Philadelphia Museum of Art.

145. RUTH HARDING
1903. 24 x 20. White House Collection. Gift of Joseph H. Hirshhorn.

146. MISS BETTY REYNOLDS
About 1903. 24 x 20. Joseph H. Hirshhorn Collection.

147. THE CORAL NECKLACE (MISS BEATRICE FENTON)
1904. 43 x 31. The Butler Institute of American Art.

148. WILLIAM R. HALLOWELL
1904. 24 x 20. Dr. Irving Levitt.

149. FRANK B. A. LINTON
1904. 24 x 20. Joseph H. Hirshhorn Collection.

150. REAR ADMIRAL GEORGE W. MELVILLE
1904. 48 x 30. Collection of the Philadelphia Museum of Art.

151. EDWARD TAYLOR SNOW
1904. 24 x 20. Collection of the Philadelphia Museum of Art.

152. WALTER MACDOWELL
1904. 27 x 20. Walter G. Macdowell.

153. EDWARD W. REDFIELD
1905. 30 x 26. National Academy of Design.

154. CHARLES L. FUSSELL
About 1905. 50 x 40. Collection of the Montclair Art Museum.

155. MRS. ELIZABETH L. BURTON
About 1905. 42 x 30. The Minneapolis Institute of Arts.

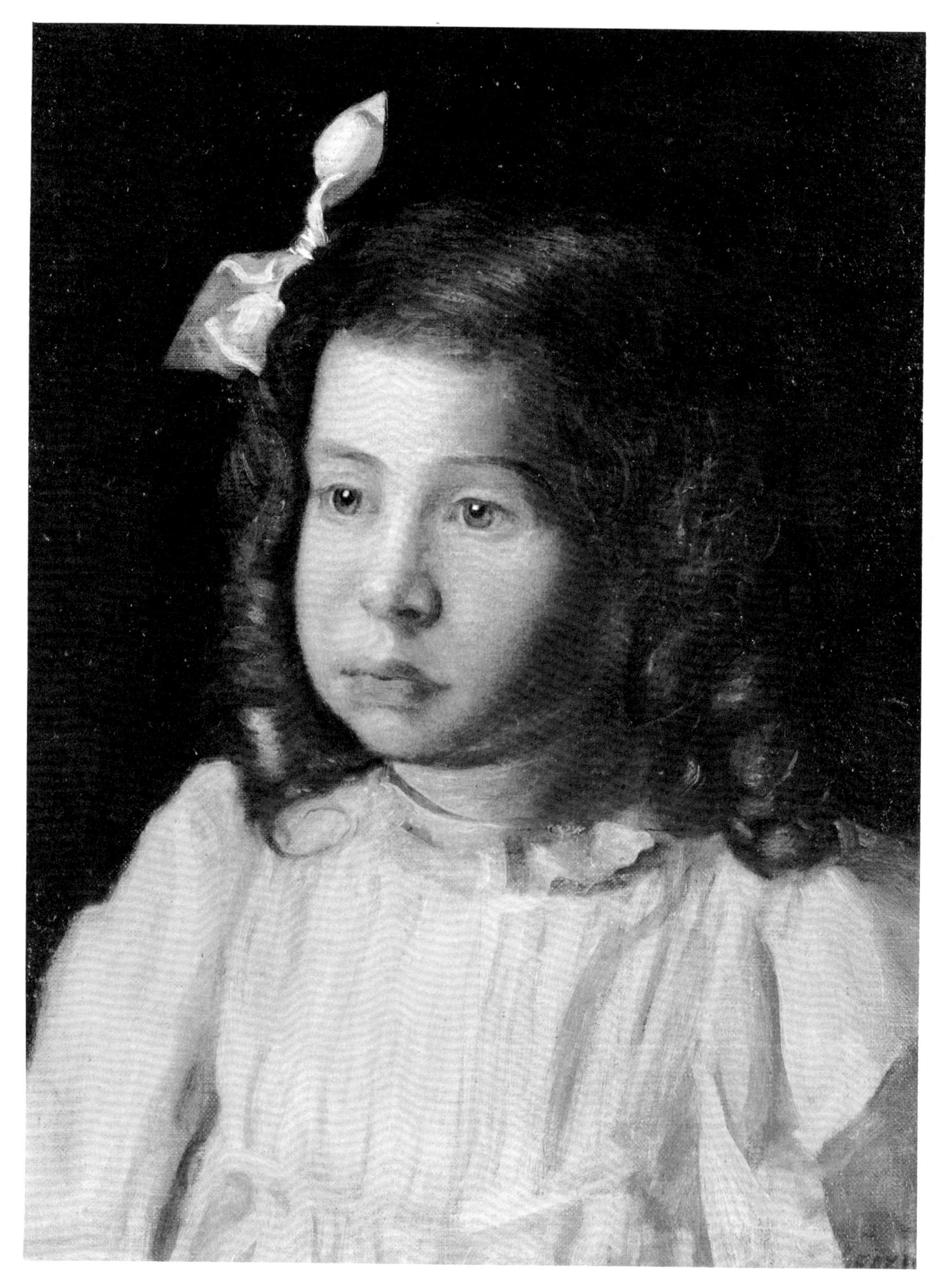

156. A LITTLE GIRL
About 1906. 16 x 12. Philadelphia Museum of Art; The Louis E. Stern Collection.

157. MRS. LOUIS HUSSON
About 1905. 24 x 20. National Gallery of Art, Washington, D.C.
Gift of Katharine Husson Horstick.

158. WILLIAM RUSH AND HIS MODEL
1908. Unfinished. 35¼ x 47½. Honolulu Academy of Arts.

Chapter Notes

Page 7:

In Eakins' time, the Pennsylvania Academy owned twenty-four portraits by Stuart. Eakins must have been impressed by Stuart's fascination with the head and by the large demonstration of style in that work. But Stuart was an unsatisfactory artist for Eakins even as a portraitist, quite apart from his abilities or inabilities as a draughtsman and colorist. Though he proposed to look at nature "for myself and see her with my own eyes," he looked primarily at heads; nature did not customarily reveal itself to him in gesture. A masterpiece like the portrait of Mrs. Richard Yates was almost unique in his work. Before Stuart, when he could avoid some of the formal necessities of commissioned work, Copley had shown some concern with the attempt to express character through psychologically expressive gesture, in *Nathaniel Hurd*, for instance, and in *Paul Revere*. But again, that kind of concern was not common in his American work.

Page 9:

"In a free and just commonwealth," Emerson wrote, "property rushes from the idle and imbecile to the industrious, brave and persevering." A corollary to this conviction was expressed by a Philadelphia minister, a contemporary of Eakins, the Reverend Russel H. Conwell (1843-1925), whose lecture "Acres of Diamonds" was delivered some six thousand times. "Money is power," he told those who wanted both. "You ought to be reasonably ambitious to have it. You ought because you can do more good with it than you could without it." This nation, under God, has in the past discovered excellent motives as it hastened to murder. Men like Conwell, no hypocrites themselves, provided, as Emerson did, justification for hordes of barbarians.

Page 10:

In the life of Clarence King, friend of Henry Adams, "the best and brightest of his generation," Van Wyck Brooks, following Adams, read "the waste of the brightest faculties unemployed by civilization, the *zeitgeist*, the time and the country." (It is of interest that in *New England: Indian Summer* Brooks has no word for Eakins, though he speaks of "the great growth of the art-schools that followed the Centennial of 1876.") The age did not favor men like King, the younger thinking men of the generation of 1870, but "the business man, the practical man and the scientific man of a practical turn who served the interests of business. . . . The commercialization of life had thinned the atmosphere. . . . The critical mind itself failed and fainted in the want of a living air to bear it up." Brook describes the mood of the *déracinés*, of the writers and intellectuals who were growing increasingly hostile to public taste, refusing to compromise with it. "Having no roots in the popular life, they were restless, cynical, sceptical, doubtful, self-conscious, apprehensive and torn by scruples . . . that devour a mind which has no large impersonal interests or any instinctive connection with primary things." Henry James ironically defined the mood of the *déraciné* in the lament of the sterile painter of "The Madonna of the Future" (1879):

> We're the disinherited of Art! We're condemned to be superficial! We're excluded from the magic circle! The soil of American perception is a poor little barren artificial deposit! Yes we're wedded to imperfection! An American, to excel, has just ten times to learn as a European! We lack the deeper sense! We have neither taste or tact nor force! How *should* we have them? Our crude and garish climate, our silent past, our deafening present, the constant pressure about us of unlovely conditions, are as void of all that nourishes and prompts and inspires the artist as my sad heart is void of bitterness in saying so! We poor aspirants must live in perpetual exile.

The comedy of this complaint lies, of course, in the self-pitying distortion of its half-truths. For, given an artist with his roots in the popular life and possessed of "the deeper sense," the taste, the fact and the force, the civilization of the Grant era and what followed *was* bound in some way to fail to sustain him.

Page 12:

For his own part, as Lloyd Goodrich observes, Eakins "read comparatively little, mostly scientific and mathematical works, scarcely ever art books or fiction, having a particularly fine scorn for French novels. . . . His tastes were independent and sure, such as his admirations for Rabelais, Dante and Whitman." He read Rabelais in French, Dante in Italian, and the Bible in the Vulgate. And throughout his life he showed an interest in language, if not in fiction.

Page 15:

"It is difficult to find anything in Eakins' art that he could have learned from Gérôme." (John Canaday, "Thomas Eakins," *Horizon*, Autumn 1964, p. 105.)

When he came upon the portrait of *Signora D'Arza (Figure 111)* hung as a pendant to the *Pygmalion and Galatea* of Gérôme in the recent-accessions room of the Metropolitan, Walter Pach felt the confrontation instructive "because it showed how a powerful personality remained untouched by bad influences." The nude in the 1877 *William Rush (Figure 34)* reminded Pach of Gérôme's

Galatea, but only for purposes of contrast. The Eakins nude was the real thing; Gérôme was Ananias, or the False Artist. It was after surveying a Gérôme nude that Henry James remarked, "Indefinable hardness is the soul of his work." Nevertheless, Eakins owed something to Gérôme's insistence upon the discovery of some inner and individual quality of the nude that would transcend classical or typical ideas of beauty. . . .

Page 16:
Gérôme's *The Execution of Marshal Ney at Luxembourg Gardens* is, in its way, a moving work. Ney lies face down in the mud before a wall whose Bonapartist slogans have been half effaced. His top hat has rolled off to the right. At the left, an officer half turns to look back as he moves away behind the firing squad marching into the dawn. Something more than its quiet anecdotal pathos very nearly redeems this work. (Sheffield City Art Galleries.)

Page 18:
Toward the end of his career Gérôme came to feel singularly out of contact with the art world; and he complained about it, in terms familiar to every age: "We are living in an age that is out of joint, in which we see the strangest things. Simplicity, naturalness, truth are no longer in fashion. We are living in a fictitious and ugly world, and I am glad that I am at the end of my career, as I would never enter those ways of which I disapprove.

"Things are seen that make reason and art shudder. . . . It might be thought that we are in an insane asylum, for it is evident to me that a breeze of insanity is blowing upon us. And works that cannot be named seem to find admirers. The more stupid a thing is, the more welcome it appears. But there is no cause to be uneasy about such productions, as they will soon pass away, for only works founded on reason are lasting." (Excerpts from letters written in 1897 and '98 are quoted and, I suppose, translated by John Sartain in his *Reminiscences.*)

Page 22:
One of the more crass views of Eakins as an objective realist can be found in Thomas Craven's *A Treasury of Art Masterpieces* (New York, 1958):

> He studied and painted many branches of sports, but enjoyed none; attended concerts to watch the performers, visited clinics and dissected corpses — and the sight of flowing blood left him unperturbed. In brief, he viewed the world as an educated observer looking for material data. Painstakingly he acquired a technique commensurate with his habits of severe calculation, and succeeded in painting, if not with passion and energy, then with extraordinary solidity and objective truth.

It was possible for one of Eakins' most responsive critics to write, in an early article, that Eakins "remained bound to the object and has not been able to go beyond it," and that "His art was lacking in the higher notes — lyricism, poetry, the natural unthinking joy in sensuous beauty. It is a Puritanical art, austere, sombre, bitter." That, interestingly, was the view of Lloyd Goodrich in the 1920's.

Later, in his book, Goodrich suggests that the aesthetic qualities of Eakins' work "were probably largely unconscious by-products of his search for truth." No, I think Eakins *began* with the search for beauty. In a letter to his father from Paris he had written: "I love sunlight and children and beautiful women and men, their heads and hands, and most everything I see, and someday I expect to paint them as I see them, and even paint some that I remember or imagine." His emotional impetus and his conscious motives are implicit here; in his painting, the quest for beauty is, to be sure, less covert in the earlier than in the later work. Somewhere among his early commentaries on Eakins, Walter Pach wrote: "There is a force in this painter that comes from his embodying . . . the character of his country and generation and such a force finds expression in relations of form and space and light that are not to be accounted for as realism."

Page 23:

Abram Lerner has said of the sketch of Margaret: "It is essentially a finished painting. The undefined vertical form to the right places Margaret's figure in space; Cezanne used the same device behind a table with apples. Spaces serve as shapes, contending with the light that is full on one side of her face. The canvas is heavily painted; paint is applied in a broken manner. Like Manet, Eakins is aware that a painting is a painting and not an attempt to fool the eye. He makes no distinction in paint in rendering the textures of background, of cloth, of flesh. The study is animated by a sense of nervous line, though the forms remain strong and simple, the treatment of dress classical, the structure of the whole important in part in countering the mood of the work, the melancholy sense of time in it created by the light, but strengthening that mood too, making it an affirmation of spirit. The portrait is as romantic as a Vuillard."

Page 37:

An early response to the effect of this painting may be found in a commentary on "American Genre Pictures" that appeared in the *New York Times* for April 20, 1879:

> The shadow of the bridge is felt although nothing more than one of the huge stone piers is visible; and if it were possible to conceive that an artist who paints like Mr. Eakins had a poetic impression, we would like to think that in this composition he had tried to express the peculiar charm that everyone has experienced when rowing out of the sunlight into the shadow of a great bridge.

When Eakins painted *The Oarsmen (Figure 123)* under a bridge two years later symbolism became submerged in the "poetic impression." The pier is a dark mass; men in a rowboat are fishing next to it. *The Pair-Oared Shell (Figure 12)* produces its effect more economically, but *The Oarsmen* achieves a richness in particularizing and drawing into its mood more of that world on a summer afternoon.

Page 40:
In the twentieth century, the closest analogy I can think of to Eakins' handling of light and time is to be found in the work of Edward Hopper where the sadness of the light and the sense of suspended time are now felt in a depersonalized world. Hopper was a great admirer of Eakins though he felt that the darkness of Eakins' canvases is "a disadvantage."

Page 50:
He continued, however, to make use of perspective sketches until almost the very last, as in the portrait of Leslie Miller (1902) *(Figure 93)* where he used one for his signature, and another, possibly, for the background. The sketch for the portrait of Miller himself was done directly with the brush and then squared off, his usual procedure with portraits. In his teaching he always laid heavy emphasis upon the mastery of perspective.

Page 55:
Rembrandt's realism was, however, in advance of his time: "Rembrandt injected into this, his first contribution to the group portrait, elements of realistic, on-the-spot observation that his predecessors in the anatomical corporation portrait had not dreamed of and that, strangely enough, even his followers seemed unable to render." (William S. Heckscher, *Rembrandt's Anatomy of Dr. Nicolaas Tulp*, New York, 1958, p. 35.)
Apart from its relationship to Rembrandt's *Anatomy*, no other possible "source" for *The Gross Clinic (Figure 22)* has been suggested. Yet at the Academy Eakins had undoubtedly seen Washington Allston's *Dead Man Restored*, a work which may have been in his mind when he conceived the sketch and worked out the completed painting.

Page 56:
The agony of the distressed mother in *The Gross Clinic (Figure 22)* is rendered in a human and understandable way though Eakins appears to have acknowledged an element of the melodramatic in her posture. In the Pennsylvania Academy archives there is a photograph of students acting out a parody of *The Gross Clinic*, with Eakins, someone has suggested, in the role of the mother.

Page 73:
An article by Gordon Hendricks in the *Bulletin* of the Philadelphia Museum of Art (Spring 1965) focuses upon the relation between Muybridge's motion photographs and Eakins' painting. Eakins' problem was "to paint, *in motion*, the coach-and-four of Fairman Rogers." In this Mr. Hendricks follows the lead of the newspaper reviews of October and November 1880 which consider Eakins' success or failure in solving that problem, and in making art of science.

Page 73:

Rogers' books included: *On Roads and Bridges* (1860); *Combinations of Mechanism Representing Mental Processes* (1874); *The Magnetism of Iron Vessels* (1877); *The Manual of Coaching* (1900).

Page 78:

Hauling the Seine (1882), another small masterpiece without the observing figures, stringing its fishermen along from the left to a more distant point along the shore, increases its distance from these men working on an overcast day. There is an almost total avoidance of naturalistic detail.

Page 81:

Academic nudes and coy maidens had been seen at the Pennsylvania Academy. Among these was Charles Leslie's copy of a nude by Benjamin West; under the title *Venus Bathing: Musidora*, it had been exhibited in 1831, and numbers of times after 1831 when it was presented by the artist to the Academy. Sully's only nude, *Musidora*, was copied from Leslie's in 1813. Another copy, finished in 1835, was eventually acquired by the Metropolitan Museum, but not exhibited by the Academy until 1922. *(American Paintings: A catalogue of the Collection of the Metropolitan Museum of Art*, 1965, I, 161, 2.)

Page 81:

Lloyd Goodrich says that Eakins' *Crucifixion* "has suggestive similarities to Ribera's *Martyrdom of St. Bartholomew* in the Prado." He is mistaken, I believe. (*Thomas Eakins: A Retrospective Exhibition*, 1961, p. 23.)

Page 87:

In the Cincinnati Museum two full-length portraits of Frank Duveneck's wife, Elizabeth Boott (the original of Pansy Osmond in *The Portrait of a Lady*), painted in the eighteen eighties, shortly after she and the artist were married, show what a relatively accomplished American artist and fond husband could do with his wife as the subject of a portrait at that time. In both these characteristically dark full-length portraits Duveneck communicates some inner quality of beauty in his wife. His feeling for her is expressed romantically, though directly and honestly enough within the idealized scheme. And yet the portraits, undoubtedly moving upon first impression, are finally deficient intellectually and imaginatively. Duveneck is unable to discover character in a beauty more typical than individual.

Page 93:

On May 1, 1879, Walter Shirlaw, writing for the Society of American Artists, complained that the Academy had disregarded the selections made by the Society's exhibition committee, in hanging a painting by Thomas Moran which had been rejected and in rejecting a work of Thomas Eakins which had been approved. The letter is of interest for it is another sign of an underlying hostility to Eakins in Philadelphia very near the beginning of his career at the Academy.

(Pennsylvania Academy Archives.) Eakins' salary in 1879 was $600 a year. It was raised after that, but he wrote in 1885 that he had never received the full amount, $2500. The promised salary, he said, had been a large factor in his remaining in Philadelphia. (Letter, Academy Archives, April 8, 1885.)

Page 93:
In an early attempt to found an academy of art in Philadelphia, Charles Willson Peale made use of a plaster cast of the *Venus de Medici* (brought to Philadelphia by Robert Edge Pine in 1784) as the nucleus of a small collection of antiques about which he built a class in drawing. Joseph Hopkinson, the author of "Hail Columbia," later recalled that the Venus "was kept *shut up in a case* and only shown to persons who wished to see it; as the manners of our country at that time would not tolerate a public exhibition of such a figure. This fact alone shows our progress in civilization and the arts." Hopkinson was not speaking in irony. Unable to find a model who would pose in the nude for his life class, Peale posed himself, though bared, it appears, only to the waist. (See Helen W. Henderson, *The Pennsylvania Academy*, Boston, 1911.)

Page 95:
Who should control an academy of art? Differing philosophies had come into conflict in the 1830's, represented by Samuel Finley Breese Morse's new National Academy and Trumbull's Academy of Fine Arts. Trumbull, a board of directors' man, saw the artist as "dependent upon the protection of the rich and the great." Morse wrote that an Academy of Arts, as he understood it, was "an institution for instruction and exhibition, exclusively under the control of artists."

George Reynolds, one of the older students at the Academy (Eakins painted him in *The Veteran* [*Figure 44*]; he had been a captain of cavalry in the Civil War), urged students "to secede from the Academy and to form a school of their own with him as the curator and with Eakins as instructor." The Art Students League was begun on the twenty-second of February, 1866, "on the second floor of a three story dwelling, the second house from the Northwest corner of Market Street and West Penn Square, where the Pennsylvania Railroad Station was later built." It later moved to 1338 Chestnut Street, a few doors from the studio (at 1310) Eakins took for a time after he married. Enrollment at the League school dwindled; numbers of students returned to the Academy, and the school went out of existence in 1892. In its earlier years the League had forty members, about twenty each in the day and the evening class. Eakins taught without pay and helped his students by paying them to pose. Franklin Schenck, whom Eakins painted numbers of times, was the League's second and last curator. (See the account of the League in Margaret McHenry, *Thomas Eakins, Who Painted*, 1946, privately printed.)

Page 95:
In the summer of 1885 Eakins was engaged in painting a picture for Edward Horner Coates of "a party of boys swimming," as Thomas Anshutz described it. On February 8, 1886, Coates wrote for the Board of Directors of the Academy

asking for Eakins' resignation as Director of the Schools of the Pennsylvania Academy. On March 12, 1886, a protest from a group of instructors at the Academy was sent to Philadelphia newspapers. The protest, "inspired by a rumor in the press that Eakins' dismissal was the result of a malicious conspiracy instead of abuse of his authority," was signed by Anshutz, among others.

(Pennsylvania Academy Archives.)

One of the most curious and unexplored aspects of Eakins' enforced resignation is hinted at in a "statement" Eakins sent to Emily Sartain in 1886, asking her to use it "in any way she thought proper."

Philadelphia
March 25, 1886

In pursuance of my business and professional studies, I use the naked model.

A number of my women pupils have for economy studied from each others' figures, and of these some have obtained from time to time my criticism on their work.

I have frequently used as models for myself my male pupils: very rarely female pupils and then only with the knowledge and consent of their mothers.

One of the women pupils, some years ago gave to her lover who communicated it to Mr. Frank Stephens a list of these pupils as far as she knew them, and since that time Mr. Frank Stephens has boasted to witnesses of the power which this knowledge gave him to turn me out of the Academy, the Philadelphia Sketch Club, & the Academy Art Club, and of his intention to drive me from the city.

Thomas Eakins

Frank Stephens (b. 1860), who had been a student at the Academy, was Eakins' brother-in-law. He had married Caroline Eakins in 1885. Stephens convinced Caroline that Eakins was taking advantage of his position at the Academy, that he was having improper relations with his students and models. Eakins' sister Frances (Crowell) apparently felt that Stephens had been unjust to her brother and the Stephens' children visited their aunt without their father until after the death of their mother and of Ella Crowell. The Crowells came to associate Eakins with Ella's insanity and her suicide in 1897 and stopped seeing him. Frank Stephens became a manufacturer of interior and exterior decoration, worked as a sculptor on the Philadelphia City Hall, and supplied decoration for the old Broad Street Station of the Pennsylvania Railroad. His terra-cotta factory, located on 48th and Girard, went out of business in 1907 and Stephens became a lecturer on art and travel. Caroline Stephens died in 1889; Stephens died June 16, 1935. (From conversation with Donald Stephens, son of Frank Stephens and Caroline Eakins Stephens.)

Page 99:
The Gilchrist portrait of Whitman is in the rare-book room of the University of Pennsylvania.

Page 103:
Though he was speaking about another portrait, that of Frank Linton *(Figure 149)*, some remarks made to me by Abram Lerner are worth quoting here because of their relevance to Eakins' feeling about the necessity to put aside "technique, rules and traditions" when painting Whitman. In the Linton portrait, Lerner sees:

> Elegance and enormous insight. Elegance in the pyramidal shape, in the line to the head, in the traditional lines of the portrait. It is like an early Manet, serious, admiring. Big drawing; he doesn't discover small complexities, but simplifies, like a sculptor, discarding, getting to the basic shape, the structure of the head. Why do the eyes have so much feeling in them? Does it all have to do with accuracy? Eakins is moved by what he sees; he never works, in this sense, from theory or style. Had he been a full professional portraitist he would have had to develop a style. Like Cezanne he depends and he does not depend upon subject matter. He is saved, I sometimes think, because he could select his models, people who interested him, as personal expressions, searching as he himself did.

Page 121:
Eakins made the heavy frame for the portrait, and marked it with the original formulas conceived by Professor Rowland. Later, when he loaned it to the Pennsylvania Academy, it was kept in the basement. "I am wondering where they have hidden my Rowland whose frame they hate but I like," Eakins wrote to Stokes in 1904. (Letter, Hirshhorn Collection.)

Page 124:
Eakins did not finish the promising full-length portrait of Mrs. Talcott Williams called *The Black Fan* (1891) *(Figure 132)*. He probably thought Mrs. Williams beautiful but Mrs. Williams did not like the shape of his vision and would not return for further sittings. She probably objected to her blotched complexion, though the biographer of Talcott Williams says that she was offended when Eakins tapped her belly and told her not to hold it in that way. *The Black Fan* and the portrait of Letitia Bacon *(Figure 53)* may be compared to William Merrit Chase's full-length *Lady with the White Shawl* (acquired by the Pennsylvania Museum in 1885), which is pretty, pleasant, painterly, and has, in fine, all the elements necessary for a small popular success at that time.

Page 130:
The genre scenes Eakins painted after his return from Dakota are strongly reminiscent of the *bodegones* of Velásquez. But they are, like the domestic genre scenes of the early eighties — *Professionals at Rehearsal* (1883) *(Figure 129)*, among them — essentially peripheral to the central interest of his work.

Page 130:

In a later portrait of a Negro, his former pupil Henry O. Tanner (1904) *(Figure 137)*, the eyes are veiled as the subject looks down. Eakins painted Negroes in the following works: *A Negress* (before 1870); *Pushing for Rail (Figure 16)*, 1874; *Whistling for Plover (Figure 17)*, 1874; *Will Schuster and Blackman (Figure 29)*, 1876; *Negro Boy Dancing*, 1878; *Shad Fishing (Figure 31)*, 1881; *Hauling Seine*, 1882; *The Red Shawl (Figure 57)*, 1890; *Henry Tanner (Figure 137)*, 1900; *William Rush (Figure 119)*, 1908. The problem was to paint the individual apart from the stereotype and behind the mask. See Sidney Kaplan's "Notes on the Exhibition" to *The Portrayal of the Negro in American Painting*, Bowdoin College, 1964. "What, indeed is more 'American,'" Kaplan asks, "than the racial tragedy — the mastered grief, the outraged stillness, the polite cynicism — that Eakins discerned in Tanner's hypersensitive face?"

Before Eakins, Copley, among others, had treated the Negro as an individual in *Watson and the Shark* (1778), in a sketch portrait (1777-83) and in *The Death of Major Peirson* (1782-84). None of these was painted in this country.

Page 132:

Whitman's death mask and a copy of it can both be found in a closet at Harvard's Houghton Library.

"Weda Cook," Goodrich writes, "remembers being in the studio when a group returned from the funeral . . . the Artist picked her up, stood her on a table, and commanded her to sing 'O Captain, My Captain'!"

Page 134:

For a review of the conditions underlying Eakins' obscurity from the late eighties on, see Goodrich, *Thomas Eakins, His Life and Work*, pp. 129-134. A brief survey of some of the more salient events of the nineties may be helpful:

1891: The directors' exhibition committee blocks the exhibition of *The Agnew Clinic (Figure 43)*. (See Eakins' letter to Edward Horner Coates, Goodrich, pp. 127, 128.)

1892: Whitman dies.

1892: The Art Students League disbands after six years.

May 1892: Eakins resigns from the Society of American Artists. (See his letter in Goodrich, pp. 130-131.)

1892, 1894: He is at work with William O'Donovan, sculpting two horses for the equestrian statues of Lincoln and Grant on the Memorial Arch, Prospect Park, Brooklyn.

1894: He delivers a lecture to the Academy of Natural Sciences and publishes his paper, "The Differential Action of Certain Muscles Passing More than One Joint."

1895: He stops lecturing on anatomy at the National Academy of Design and at Drexel Institute.

1896: Eakins' only one-man exhibition takes place at the Earle Galleries in Philadelphia.
1897: Eakins' niece Ella Crowell kills herself after a period of illness.
1898: He delivers the last of his lectures at Cooper Union.
December 30, 1899: Benjamin Eakins dies.

At some time in the nineties, Eakins aids Samuel Murray in sculpting the prophets, formerly on the Witherspoon Building at Walnut and Juniper streets in Philadelphia. (See McHenry, *Thomas Eakins, Who Painted*, pp. 127-128.)

The conclusion to his 1894 lecture is worth quoting once more. It is more than it appears and more than a mere statement of intention over a lifetime: "One is never sure he understands the least movement of an animal, unless he can connect it with the whole muscular system, making, in fact, a complete circuit of all the strains. The differential muscles once understood, it is less difficult to connect nearly all the other great muscles with the principal movement of the animal, that of progression in the horse, and to understand, roughly, the combinations necessary for other movements.

"On the lines of the mighty and simple strains dominating the movement, and felt intuitively and studied out by him, the master artist groups with full intention, his muscular forms. No detail contradicts. His men and animals live. Such is the work of three or four modern artists. Such was the work of many an old Greek sculptor."

Page 142:

When Hamilton lamented the neglect of Eakins in his autobiography, it came as a footnote to his praise of Edward Horner Coates. "The reign of Mr. Coates at the Academy marked the period of its greatest prosperity. . . . Two of the greatest masterpieces of American art were produced — *The Clinic of Doctor Gross* and *The Clinic of Doctor Agnew*, by Thomas Eakins — rare works that carry on the best traditions of the masters. Unfortunately . . . these pictures are hidden away. . . ." (*Men I Have Painted*, 1921, p. 178.)

Hamilton's *Gladstone at Downing Street* was purchased for the Pennsylvania Academy in 1894. The portrait shows Gladstone reading in his library. The elements of its informal realism are not ordered by a powerful intellect. Its details distract, and it conveys no force of insight. As an example of the aesthetic deficiencies of a kind of portraiture that was successful in its time, it may be compared with one of Eakins' few large failures, his portrait of Riter Fitzgerald (1895) *(Figure 61)*. Yet the Fitzgerald, though overlarge and loose, has a life in it that the Gladstone lacks.

Page 145:

Eakins had been a frequent guest at the home of James Mapes Dodge where he attended musical recitals. He is said to have been so moved by passages in

Brahms and Beethoven that he would sit alone in a corner and weep during a performance.

Page 145:

Born in 1841, Emily Sartain was three years older than Eakins. Her brother William was in Eakins' graduating class at Central High School in 1861. Her father, John Sartain (1808-1897), was a man of great energy, an engraver of prodigious output who produced some of the finest mezzotints ever executed in America, and an architectural designer (he was responsible for the arrangement of the galleries at the Pennsylvania Academy) as well as an editor and publisher. It was Sartain who, during his association with *Graham's* magazine after 1841, made pictorial illustration a distinctive feature of American periodicals. *Sartain's Union Magazine of Literature and Art* (1849-1852) had its own importance in the history of American culture.

In 1866 Sartain wrote a letter for Eakins recommending him to Gérôme. After that, although Eakins had known the Sartain family from his earliest childhood, there are numbers of indications (especially from 1879 on) that Sartain did not like him. Had Eakins ever given Miss Emily false reason to hope that he might marry her? During his first year in Paris he had written her numbers of letters which imply a relationship that had once been closer. Now they engage in mildly intellectual contention with distinct emotional undertones, as when he defines politeness, apparently in answer to a charge. "If by politeness then is meant goodness, it is appreciated by me as I trust it always has been, but if it is to mean the string of ceremonies generally used for concealing ill nature, and which have been found necessary to the existence of every society whose members are wanting in self respect and morality, I detest it more than ever.

"My prominent idea of a polite man is one who is nothing but polish. It is an unenviable reputation. If there was anything else in him the polish would never be noticed. He is a bad drawing finely worked up, and Gérôme says that every attempt at finish on a bad design serves only to make the work more contemptible."

In another letter he defends himself against her charge that he is hard and cynical. Some years later, writing to Susan Macdowell (September 9, 1879) Eakins tells her: "I am just going to Newport. I learned this morning that the Directors on the recommendation of the Committee on Instruction have appointed me Professor of Drawing and Painting. They did this last night and Mr. Rogers wanted me to wait here so as to give the first lesson. I found 4 antique fellows whom I instructed and introduced to Billy Sartain whom I substitute [sic] till I come back.

"When old Sartain learns not only that I have the place, but that the other young firebrand Billy is keeping it for me, I fear his rage may bring on a fit."

It should be observed that as chief of the Bureau of Art for the Centennial Exhibition, Sartain must have played a role in placing *The Gross Clinic* in the Exhibition's medical section. Further, as chief of the American art department for a London exhibition in 1886, he chose no work by Eakins. Sartain was one of the directors at the Pennsylvania Academy at the time of Eakins' resignation. He made no reference to Eakins in his *Reminiscences* (1899).

Page 161:

Though Barnes made news when he purchased the portrait sketch of Dr. Agnew *(Figure 42)* for something less than five thousand dollars he did not, on the whole, have a high opinion of Eakins. "Eakins," he wrote, "was able to make a fairly personal and competent use of the great Dutch and Spanish traditions as given a modern version by Manet. . . . Eakins was essentially a school painter who created nothing truly original; but he had such a fine feeling for composition, for the relation of objects to each other, and such command of the medium of paint, that his works are personal expressions even though they are not creations of the first rank. The portrait of Dr. Agnew . . . illustrates well his ability to render convincing solidity, poised movement, and effective space-relations with great skill. It shows the essentials of his subject, including character and dignity. His limited palette in this picture gives the effect of economy and subtlety, but in his average work it seems merely to indicate poverty of resources. In the majority of his paintings, the tight drawing, the inadequate feeling for color, and the stereotyped quality of his themes, relegates him to the status of the skilled academician."

Barnes did not know the great body of Eakins' work. He had some interest in American art, in Glackens and in other members of the Eight, and later in Pippens. He also collected American furniture.

Page 162:

George Biddle and Nathaniel Burt are among the many who have written of the less than satisfactory relationship between the artist and his public in Philadelphia. In the thirties Biddle observed that "Philadelphia has relentlessly hated ideas and consequently disliked artists. Artists have in the main reciprocated and have run away." Nathaniel Burt's more recent analysis remains in essential agreement. "There are few if any American cities where the connections between art and the aristocrat have been so close, not always to their mutual benefit. Yet in general, there is no place where the arts are or have been regarded with less real esteem."

By "Philadelphia" Biddle meant of course the class of Philadelphians that he had deserted. It is possible to believe, however, that the old attitudes are changing as new collectors enter the field and new ranks of "aristocrats" form themselves.

Page 165:

The writing master's charge for lettering a diploma in 1883 was forty cents. An account book for the period in Eakins' handwriting can be found at the Pennsylvania Historical Society.

Page 172:

a. The portrait of Macdowell in a large hat *(Figure 79)* was probably influenced by either or both of the Rembrandt portraits of men in large hats acquired by the Metropolitan Museum in 1890 and 1891. Although the photograph Eakins took of Macdowell at about this time may have been used for the portrait, he continued to work primarily from the life.

b. Macdowell's great hero was Tom Paine.

Page 192:

Kenton had married Elizabeth Macdowell, Eakins' sister-in-law, a painter of some talent, a contentious woman of great spirit, and a more than ordinarily troublesome wife. She and Kenton eventually separated.

Page 192:

Sheeler's later opinion was that "unlike Eakins, Rembrandt imposes his own terms upon nature. Eakins had a sense of craft but it was mainly clinical. Somewhere there was an emotional element but he seldom got around to reveal it. He never let us share the sense of beauty which he may have seen in these homely characters. The great realist offers a final enhancement. . . . We get his vision of the facts as well as the facts."

Page 200:

The full-length portrait of Archbishop James Frederick Wood *(Figure 96)* was painted in 1877. Thirty-five years ago, Lloyd Goodrich found it in bad condition, much darkened. Since then it has been restored. The Archbishop shows us the face of a kindly old man, a brown benevolence, the wisdom of age. It is not easy for an observer to say how much of the original portrait remains, yet there is enough to see that it was an impressive work in the grand manner which could in itself have established Eakins' reputation.

The study for this portrait is small and hard, reflecting the manner of Gérôme more than the mature early style of Eakins, who had produced a freer study in the head of Dr. Gross a year before. The Archbishop has a pained look and a squint, as if he were looking into the light. Eakins records the droop of an eyelid and the row of hard red buttons down the front of his robe *(Figure 95)*.

Page 200:

Goodrich had been unable to find the Garvey portrait. Eakins' inscription for it on the back of the canvas, reads:

Reverendum Dom^{vm}
PATRITIUM GARVEY S.T.D.
RECTOREM SEINARII
S^{TI} CAROLI
APVD OVERBROOK
VIVVM DEPINXIT
Thomas Eakins
ADMCMII

Page 226:

In October 1965 I visited Mrs. John B. Whiteman, whose portrait Eakins had also painted in 1903, the "head and bust," as Goodrich describes it, "of a young woman of about twenty, slightly left of full face, looking down to the left. Brown hair, tanned face, bare throat and arms; low necked cream colored dress, with a flounce of deep lace around front and shoulders." Benjamin Eakins had been her father's writing teacher; her mother and father had met in the Macdowell home, and Thomas Eakins attended her wedding to John Whiteman. Eakins spent a good part of the summer of 1903 working at her portrait. He did not photograph her. She had been playing tennis that summer in a long-sleeved high-necked blouse which she removed when she posed for him; her arms and neck were pale, her face sunburned, and he painted her that way.

"Mr. Eakins," she told him during one sitting, "my collar button has gone down my back and it hurts sitting here." He reached down to retrieve it, and told her, "Your back is more like a boy's than a girl's." He told her he would like to paint her in the nude, and she said she would ask her mother about it. Her mother said it would be perfectly all right if she did. "Tom is an old fool about the nude. He would look at you as if you were an anatomical specimen." But she thought it would be just as well not to, and Eakins did not ask her again. Eakins gave her the portrait; her parents did not like it. "My neck bones show in it. 'You look like a bag of bones, like an anatomical sketch,' they said. They thought it was hideous, that I looked like a boy, with a beard coming." She sat an hour or two for Frederick Waugh at about the same time; the girl in Waugh's portrait is much prettier in a conventional way.

To entertain her during her rest periods Eakins played translation games using an Italian newspaper. He also taught her a song that he had learned during his student days in Paris; she recalled it in this way, with triple repetitions of one word or syllable in each line, and I record it as she remembered it:

Il était un petit navire
Qui n'était (ja ja) jamais navigé.
Il entrepris un long voyage
Sur le côte (côte côte) d'Avigné.
Après cinq (cinq cinq) ou six semaines
Les vivres vinrent a manqué.
Ils tirent les longues pailles
Pour savoir qui (qui qui) serait manger.
Le sort tomba sur le plus jeune
Avec sauce blanche il fut mangé.

The portrait of Elizabeth Burton (about 1905) *(Figure 155)* is another in which it is difficult to read the themes we associate with Eakins in the late portraits — weariness or resignation, bitterness or disappointment or suffering. The naturalist whose total experience convinces him of the inevitable sadness of life can yield to the romantic who sees a gallantry in the assertion of spirit or of will. There is maturity, intelligence, sadness in that young face, but these are countered by the dramatic posture and by the richness of her dress, implying a vitality that has not yielded to life. I am reminded of other portraits, of men, in which traits of character seem more important than the lessons of existence — the pensive quality allied something like arrogance in Kern Dodge *(Figure 141)*, or to the hard, cold, iron stoicism of Admiral Melville *(Figure 150)*.

Page 232:

This may seem a peculiar statement given the work of Cole, of Asher Durand, Doughty, the early Church, the Hudson River painters and other greater and lesser painters of American landscape. The romantic realists painted specific places, surely, but in their distant views, or in their naturalistic handling of tree and foliage where is the American fact? It dissolves in the grandeur of nature, in the sought romantic effects. One of the interests of Cole's *The Ox-Bow* is its specificity in the self-portrait of the artist with his materials in the midst of that grandeur. We rightly value these men, but there is another sort of mind at work when Eakins places himself and others in the landscapes around Philadelphia.

Page 235:

"It is as though Eakins were painting his personal comment on the creative act. There is in these pictures a disturbing sense of unreality. Are they not perhaps, after all, dream images? For this is not realism in art, but rather the art of giving tangible form to a vision." (James W. Fosburgh, "Music and Meaning: Eakins' Progress," *Art News*, February 1958.)

Page 235:

Among other honors, he served as a juror for the Carnegie International Exhibition for a number of years. But even there his work was not always accepted. *Cowboys at the Home Ranch* was rejected in 1896, *The Art Student* and *The Violinist* in 1904, *William Rush Carving the Allegorical Figure of the Schuylkill* in 1908, and portraits in 1909, 1911, and 1913 were not accepted. The Exhibition did accept other works in some of the same years: *The Writing Master*, 1896, *Mrs. Frishmuth*, 1904; *Portrait of a Clergyman*, 1908, and *Louis Husson*, 1911. (The portrait of Miss Coffin was rejected in that year.) On the whole the record of acceptance was good; it also included the following: *Rail Shooting* (1896), *Professor Culin* (1899), *Salutat* (1899), *Chase* (1899), *The Crucifixion* (1900), *Louis Kenton* (1900), *Henry Rowland* (1901), *Cardinal Martinelli* and *The Oboe Player* (1903), *Charles Fussell* and *Admiral Melville* (1905), *Leslie Miller* (1907), *Edward Schmidt* (1910), and *Mrs. Gilbert Lafayette Parker* (1912).

Page 238:

One of the more sensitive of Eakins' present-day critics has asked whether Eakins might one day have a larger more appreciative audience than he has today: "One wonders if the present mood of America with its large enthusiasm for synthetic emotions and merchandised pieties glorifying distractions and avoiding issues may be any more auspicious for Eakins than his own time. He may be still too thoroughgoing, too radical, too genuine." The writer's hope that "the nation that produced him may one day catch up with him" is very American, and very much apart from reality. (Leslie Katz, "Thomas Eakins Now," *Arts*, September 1956.)

Index

Note: Page numbers in italics refer to illustrations.